No Place Left Called Home

D1025233

No Place Left Called Home

by James A. Cogswell

Friendship Press, New York

Library of Congress Cataloging in Publication Data

Cogswell, James A.
    No Place Left Called Home.

    Includes bibliographical references.
    1. Homelessness – United States.   2. Refugees – United States.
    3. Homelessness – Canada.   4. Refugees – Canada.   I. Title.
HV4493.C63
ISBN 0-377-00128-7   362.5'1 0973   82-24215

Unless otherwise stated, all Bible quotations used in this book are from the Revised
Standard Version, copyright 1946 and 1952, by the Division of Christian Education
of the National Council of the Churches of Christ in the United States of America.

Copyright © 1983 by Friendship Press, Inc.
Printed in the United States of America
Editorial Office: 475 Riverside Drive, Room 772, New York, NY 10115
Distribution Office: P.O. Box 37844, Cincinnati, OH 45237

Contents

INTRODUCTION

It happened on a Sunday morning as one congregation worshiped. The time had come to express concerns and celebrations. One prayer request was for a delegation from Church World Service which included a friend of many in the congregation. The group was at that time visiting refugee camps in East Africa and would soon travel to refugee centers in Europe. The congregation asked that the delegation be sustained in this overwhelming experience and that through them the church in their home nation would grow in its compassion for the millions of refugees around the world.

"Speaking of refugees," the next person said, "the Vietnamese family sponsored by our church is at a critical point. The father has worked hard to get training as a computer technician, but he can't find a job. Let's pray for them."

"And speaking of refugees," another person added, "we had quite an experience yesterday. As we were cleaning the church building, we found that a runaway teenage couple had been living for several days in the furnace room. We took them to get help. Let's pray for them."

A fourth voice picked up the cue. The person requesting prayer was a member of a team about to begin a ministry called "Open Door" in the inner city. The new work was intended to reach street people who have no home, who exist from meal to meal, who often must sleep in the open even in the dead of winter. The congregation was encouraged to pray for this ministry.

Yet another voice was heard, that of the director of a home for the elderly. "Many of the people in our retirement home have no close relatives, no place to turn in case of adversity. They are feeling the effect of inflation. Their pensions and retirement incomes are becoming extremely strained. What are they to do? Please pray for them."

The morning prayer became one church community's struggle to comprehend the agony of the world's uprooted persons, many far removed from the church members but many right at their doorsteps.

To say that rootlessness is a characteristic of these times is to state the obvious. Most people realize how shallow their own roots are.

How many places have you lived? The average American changes homes 13 times during his/her life! How long, on an average, have you lived in one place?

The people of North America are rightly characterized as members of mobile societies. Yet there is a marked difference between being mobile and being uprooted. For many, mobility is voluntary. They move in order to take advantage of greater opportunities—better income, more favorable climate, more comfortable homes. This is often "upward mobility."

But for the world's uprooted persons, the jerking up of roots is usually traumatic, even violent. They must pass into a valley of the shadow of death, with no certainty whatsoever about home, about land, about livelihood, about life itself. Fortunate indeed are those who find home or land or livelihood on the other side of that valley. Many, however, will live the rest of their days in the valley and will die as uprooted persons.

The most stark expression of the uprootedness of these times is the increasing tide of refugees. The United Nations High Commissioner for Refugees estimates that since World War II more than 25 million persons have fled their homelands to seek refuge in another place.

The plight of persons who are the world's uprooted presents a monumental challenge to Christian faith. Christians need the full resources of their biblical and theological heritage to know how to cope, to interpret, to respond, to be faithful; therefore that is the place where this study begins. (Chapter 1)

The next task in this book is to gain a better understanding of the global refugee situation, to enter into its agony through the experience of individual people, to probe the depths of those volcanic forces which are uprooting and spewing people across the earth, and to consider the ethical issues confronting Christians. (Chapter 2)

How do North Americans respond to the plight of these uprooted persons? North America has a history which provokes both pride and shame. Attitudes have swung like a pendulum between hospitality and hostility. North Americans are at a time in their national lives when the "gangplank mentality" is growing. This sentiment is increasing, moving to wall off the seas of agony that beat upon Fortress America. What are just and sane immigration policies for the United States and

2

Canada to follow in such a time as this? They must include a realistic assessment as to what portion of the world's uprooted people can be received into the United States and Canada. But beyond that root causes must be addressed and those systems changed which create this great tide of displaced people. (Chapter 3)

As the human family seeks to understand the uprootedness of so many in this time, one evident cause is the accelerating pace of loss of land among rural poor people. As the world's limited arable land is increasingly controlled by national elite and multinational corporations, low-income rural people are being uprooted from lands that they had farmed for generations. Some push or are pushed across national boundaries to become part of the tide of international migration.

Many more remain within their country. They become what is often viewed as a mass of indigestible poverty, forming hungry necklaces around the edges of Third World cities. But these masses are individuals, persons in need of roots. Certain Third World countries, such as the Philippines and El Salvador, present glaring examples of the plight of the landless. U.S. and Canadian citizens must confront the same phenomenon within their own national life, in the rural South, among Native Americans, among farmers in Saskatchewan and in Appalachia. How do Christians stand with the uprooted rural poor in their struggle for land and self-determination? (Chapter 4)

Another side of this coin is unemployment. Uprooted persons somehow must survive, seeking jobs wherever they can. The alarming unemployment rate in low-income countries will inevitably push the more ambitious across national borders to richer countries, seeking a livelihood and a "way out."

For people in the United States, the Third World presses upon their southern border. In spite of the many attempts made by policies on paper, it has been virtually impossible to stem the tide of jobless individuals who seek only a chance to "make it" by doing menial jobs at lowest wages. The growing number of migrants from Mexico and other countries . . . the legal and illegal . . . the periodic bursts of Cuban immigration . . . the desperate efforts of Haitians to make it to U.S. shores . . . how do people in the United States and Canada deal with the world's jobless? How are their desperate needs weighed against those of the unemployed already living within U.S. and

Canadian borders? How do the world's jobless challenge those with jobs to think creatively about the global community? (Chapter 5)

But concern about uprooted persons "out in the world" will be hollow and shallow indeed unless the reality of the uprooted in our own communities is confronted. Some of these persons are victims of those same forces which have created uprootedness in the rest of the world, including loss of land and factory closings. Others pay the price for "progress." These persons with low incomes are often displaced by "urban renewal." Some are part of the "turned-off, dropped-out" generation, who have left home and family and now long for a place to put down roots. Others have become street people whose daily goal is simply finding food to eat and a place to sleep. Some may be the family members, close or distant relatives, of the rooted, secure persons who surround them. Possibly they are the elderly men and women who have been uprooted from home, loved ones, neighborhood and all that they had known and loved, who yearn for some sense that they have a place called home. What is the calling of Christians in relation to uprooted persons in their own home towns? (Chapter 6)

Learning about uprootedness is not a one-way street. There is much to be learned from the world's uprooted people. Such an exchange within the human community renews a vision of what God is up to in history and enables the world community to discover and rediscover common roots. The human family might then become a whole community. (Chapter 7)

That indeed would make whatever is done with and on behalf of uprooted persons well worth every effort.

Chapter One:
Christian Roots and
Uprooted People

Abraham and Sarah were always living on somebody else's land! From the moment they left the highly developed urban civilization of Ur of the Chaldees (Gen. 12:1-3), they took up once again the nomadic life of their forebears, living in the light of a promise. They became "sojourners," lacking the protections provided by family and birthplace, dependent upon the hospitality of others. Their sojourn led them to different places where they received differing receptions. (Gen. 12:10-20; 20:1-18; 21:25-34)

When Isaac left the land in which he sojourned (Gen. 26:1-16), Rebekah left her home and became a sojourner. Isaac had sojourned to Rebekah's homeland when he was searching for a bride. She left her homeland and became a sojourner when he returned to his roots. Jacob likewise was a sojourner. (Gen. 32:4; 36:6-7)

The Hebrew people were exhorted never to forget that their ancestors were sojourners. They sang about it in their psalms (Ps. 39:12; 105:6-15); they rehearsed it in their ceremonies. (Deut. 26:1-5) They were to treat justly and compassionately those who sojourned among them, remembering that they were descendants of sojourners. (Exod. 22:21; 23:9; Lev. 19:33-34; Deut. 10:19; 24:17-22)

Think about your own heritage. What are your roots through your father? Your mother? When did your ancestors come to this continent? Why? How long were they "sojourners" before becoming citizens?

THE NEED FOR "A PLACE TO BE"

The yearning for roots in one's own place and land speaks to the heart of every person. Paul Tournier, the French psychologist/theologian, describes it poignantly in his book, *A Place for*

You. A young student told Tournier of his difficulties, of an anxiety that never left him, at times turning to panic and flight. The student summed up his feelings, "Basically, I'm always looking for a place—for somewhere to be."

Tournier expounds upon this insight, explaining that to have strong roots in one's own place is to be better able to enter into real communion with all other places in the world. To be denied a place is to suffer a serious trauma, a denial of one's own humanity. To be uprooted is to be torn away from the love of neighbors and to lose one's place in the world. All those shuttled from one place to another by the changes and chances of life can echo the words of one poet, "To depart is to die a little."[1]

The trauma of uprootedness is something most persons have known to some degree. The uprootedness may have affected them slightly or severely. It may be that their lives continue to reflect the impact of the uprootedness of past generations. Alex Haley's popular story *Roots* has renewed in many black citizens in the United States a sense of pride in their origins. It also has deepened their understanding of the psychological injury inflicted for generations by violent uprooting.

One of the recurring themes of history is the itinerant nature of the human race, but this era is particularly characterized by involuntary, violent population upheaval. Within this century, individuals, families, tribes, ethnic groups, communities and even whole nations have been forced to move for political, economic and religious reasons. At the same time, within the communities and regions of North America, many are uprooted from home, job, neighborhood—from their "place to be."

How do members of the Christian community deal with this? As human beings? As Christians? How do Christians respond in ways that do more than treat symptoms or salve consciences, in ways that address solutions? How can Christians give themselves to a struggle that most likely will not achieve "success" in their lifetimes?

These are faith questions. And they drive Christians to the source of their faith. Biblical themes and theological convictions will light this complex, but critically important, study.

SOME BIBLICAL THEMES

God is the Sovereign Ruler of creation. Self-evident, it seems, yet very, very important. The Bible affirms that God is the source and sustainer of all that is. Paul wrote that God works all things after the counsel of God's will. (Eph. 1:11) The community of faith would say human history is not simply a chaotic series of events without meaning or purpose. As tragic and meaningless as much human suffering can be, God is working out God's purpose, in the middle of and even through suffering.

Human life and action are often shaped by rejection of that divine purpose. History often reflects human injustice, misery and exploitation rather than divine justice and righteousness. Again, in the words of Paul, "all have sinned and come short of the glory of God." (Rom. 3:23)

The human story is one of constant struggle and tension between finding roots in true community and being uprooted because of sinfulness. The Garden of Eden story is everyone's story. That lovely oasis possessed food in abundance, cool shade, gentle winds, life-giving water and continuing fellowship with God. That oasis is the place now barred to humankind because of rebellion against God's purpose and confidence in human power, human will, human design.

One of the most striking manifestations of this rebellion is the treatment of other human beings. Attitudes toward others are always linked to the worship of and attitude toward God. So Cain, having slain his brother Abel, is condemned to be a "fugitive and wanderer on the earth" (Gen. 4:12), dwelling in "the land of Nod (wandering)," now a symbol for the dwelling place of all human beings removed from their true "home" which is with God.

Yet God's intention continues that earth be "home" for everyone. "The earth is the Lord's and the fullness thereof," sings the Psalmist, "the world and they that dwell therein." (Ps. 24:1) (KJV)

This conviction that "the world is made for everyone" is well expressed by the statement of the Second Vatican Council:

"God intended the earth and all that it contains for the use of every human being and people. Thus, as all people follow justice and unite in charity, created goods should abound for them on a reasonable basis . . . . The right to have a share of earthly goods sufficient for oneself and one's family belongs to everyone.''

A basic theme in the story of God's chosen people is that being "rooted" is a sign of God's blessing on the righteous. (Ps. 1; Prov. 12:3,12) Uprooting signified God's judgment upon the Israelites' unfaithfulness. (Deut. 29:24-28; 1 Kings 14:15; Ps. 52:1-5) While Israel may pass through judgment and be uprooted, God's ultimate intention is for God's people to be rooted again. (Isa. 27:6; Hos. 14:5-6; Amos 9:15)

The prophets added a new dimension to this analogy. They saw how some who appear to be well-rooted are wicked (Jer. 12:1-2) and how they in turn may uproot others. (Mic. 2:1-2; Isa. 5:8) Uprootedness, then, is not in and of itself a sign of God's judgment, but rather may be a manifestation of the inhumanity of persons to one another.

The story of the Exodus manifests on a grand scale God's design. God's plan was to uproot people out of slavery and oppression and plant them again where their whole life may glorify God. God especially loves and cares for the poor and oppressed, and uproots them in order to deliver them. (Exod. 6:5-8) While God's providential care was with the Israelites in the perils of their wilderness wandering, the ultimate purpose was to plant them again that they might bear fruit to the glory of God. (Deut. 4:32-40)

The liberation that God wrought for the people of Israel became the touchstone by which they lived and became a nation. God's people were to recognize the rights of the poor people. Poor persons were not to be simply the objects of people's pity, but were to be protected by law from exploitation. (Exod. 22:25-27; Lev. 19:9-10, 13-15; 25:35-38; Deut. 24:17-22)

This protection of those who were poor applied particularly to the land in which they were rooted. "No land shall be sold outright," said the law, "because you do not own it; it belongs to God, and you are like foreigners who are allowed to make use of it." (Lev. 25:23) The land could be leased, or given out as security for a loan, but on the jubilee year, the land was to revert to the original family. This was to insure that none would be permanently poverty-stricken, and all could live in the expectation of making a fresh start. (Lev. 25:8-10)

The "stranger" or "sojourner" was to be given the same protection as Israel's poor. Not only did Israelites see themselves as a "wandering" and "sojourning" nation, but throughout much of their history, there were non-Israelite persons within Israel's borders. These persons were called strangers, sojourners, aliens and foreigners. Many became incorporated into the life of the nation and functioned to all intents and purposes as citizens of Israel. Such persons were free to embrace the faith of Israel if they wished and were, in any case, expected to live by the laws of Israel.

These persons, in turn, were to be accorded the full rights and protection of the law. (Lev. 24:22) They were entitled to the same basic though rudimentary provision for survival as the poor. (Lev. 23:22) The sojourner was to be paid promptly and fairly for labor. (Deut. 24:14-15) Thus the God who saved Israel from bondage was seen as the protector of all who were poor, weak, disinherited and strangers and Israel was to reflect that love. (Exod. 23:9; Deut. 10:17-19)

Disobedience to God's passion for justice would lead to uprooting and captivity. The prophets announced that God's justice was a two-edged sword. When the people of Israel were oppressed, their oppression eventually led to their freedom. When they became oppressors, their oppression of others led to their uprooting. The explosive message of the prophets is that God destroyed Israel and sent the people of Judah into captivity because of their mistreatment and exploitation of persons who were poor and strangers among them. (Amos 6:1-7; Isa. 3:13-15; 5:1-7; 10:1-4; Mic. 6:9-13; Jer. 5:26-29) The heartrending grief of the Hebrew exiles, their nostalgia for Jerusalem, for the temple, for their ravaged homeland, expresses in universal language the distress of the uprooted. (Ps. 137)

Yet God's purpose is not to condemn but to redeem. The Psalmist looked to a future in which Israel would be restored and justice for the poor would prevail, through the coming of the One who would establish justice. (Ps. 72) Prophets proclaimed the hope of a future messianic rule brought by one who would spring from the "root of Jesse," when peace, righteousness and justice would abound in a new society. (Isa. 11:1-10; 61:1-11; Jer. 23:5-6)

The coming of Jesus brings good news to persons who are poor, who are held captive, who are oppressed. Jesus' coming was seen as the fulfillment of the hope proclaimed by the prophets for one who would "put down the mighty from their thrones and exalt those of low degree . . . fill the hungry with good things and send the rich away empty." (Luke 1:52-53)

Jesus defined his own mission in words that throb with hope for poor and oppressed persons.

"The Spirit of the Lord is upon me, because He has anointed me to preach good news to the poor, to proclaim release to the captives and recovering of sight to the blind, to set at liberty those who are oppressed, to proclaim the acceptable year of the Lord." (Luke 4:18-19)

The Gospels attest that Jesus spent much of his life as one "uprooted." Born in a borrowed stable (Luke 2:7), the infant Jesus was taken by his family as a refugee into Egypt to escape the death threat of Herod. (Matt. 2:13-15) Jesus spent his ministry on the move, as one who had no place to lay his head. (Matt. 8:20; Luke 9:58) He identified himself with the poor and called upon his disciples to do the same, casting themselves upon the compassion of the community into which they came. (Luke 9:3-5; 10:3-11)

Jesus identifies himself with the world's uprooted. For Christians, being confronted with the uprooted is being confronted with Christ. In the famous portrayal of the Last Judgment in Matthew 25:31-46, Jesus identifies himself as the person who is hungry, thirsty, a stranger, naked, ill or held prisoner. All are refered to as Christ's brothers and sisters on the basis of common need rather than national or religious origin. In caring for Jesus' own, Christians are accepting or rejecting Christ himself. In this startling and complete identification with the strangers, Jesus founds a radical new relationship, that of "neighbor."[2]

Christians are called to share Christ's concern for the uprooted. The New Testament abounds, in exhortations to the early Christians to express hospitality to strangers. (Heb. 13:2; Rom. 12:13; 1 Tim. 3:2; 5:10; Titus 1:8; 1 Pet. 4:9) Hospitality literally meant, "receiving the outsider." This hospitality was especially to be extended to those in "the household of faith" (Acts 16:15; 18:27; 3 John 5), and was indeed the primary bond that unified the early churches. Yet, the hospitality was to extend beyond those bounds. Christians were to remember that they also were once "separated from Christ, alienated from the commonwealth of Israel, and strangers to the covenant of promise," but now had "been brought near in the blood of Christ." (Eph. 2:11-13) The presence of Jew and Gentile together in the early Christian community was evidence of the fact that in Christ "you are no longer strangers and sojourners, but fellow citizens with the saints and members of the household of God.'' (Eph. 2:19)

Christians share a vision of the kingdom of God which makes them live as strangers and pilgrims on the earth. Political and geographical boundaries are part of the human social order which have their meaning for their time. (Num. 34; Ezek. 48) But such borders become secondary as Christians see God's intention to assure life, peace, justice and well-being for the earth's total human community.

"Kingdom" was a contemporary image for socio-political realities in Israel. For Christians today, the "kingdom" of God might be more appropriately called the community of the sovereign God. This community, Jesus proclaimed, surpasses all human boundaries. (Luke 13:29; Matt. 8:11-12) Indeed, eventually those boundaries will fade away before the reality of God's coming community. (Rev. 11:15)

Christians therefore now live in tension as citizens of earthly political systems and citizens of the coming community of the sovereign God. (Phil. 3:20) They sense themselves to be strangers and pilgrims on the earth with their eyes set on a better country. (Heb. 11:13-16) With that vision before them, Christians offer their strength to struggle "against the principalities and powers, against the world rulers of this present darkness.'' (Eph. 6:22)

Christians look toward an end to those divisions of humankind which set people against one another. (Gal. 3:26-28; 1 Cor. 12:12-13) Indeed, Christians see the ultimate goal as reconciling all those things in Christ. (Col. 1:19-20; Eph. 1:9-10) This vision of one human family beckons the church forward. In this vision all members of the world community will have the opportunity to live truly human lives, responding to the purposes of God.

SOME THEOLOGICAL CONVICTIONS

Out of this brief recounting from the biblical story, certain convictions become the basis for dealing with the problems of the world's uprooted people.

Christians are called to compassion for those who suffer. The normative response of Christians to those who suffer is compassion. Compassion is being so moved by the suffering of another that the core of personhood is affected. Compassionate persons can do nothing other than respond to suffering. The model of compassionate response for Christians is Jesus. Moved by the brokenness of individuals, Jesus healed. (Mark 1:41; 5:19; 7:13; Matt. 20:34) Moved by the needs of the masses, Jesus responded with merciful action. (Matt. 9:36; 10:14; 15:32)

As Christians encounter persons who are experiencing hardship, the compassionate response cannot be criticism, accusation or condemnation. Nor does compassion permit a paternalistic response in which a relationship of "superior-inferior" is implied. It is rather a heartfelt response that emerges out of an equal relationship as persons in God's family. Christians respond to suffering because the human family is united, created in the image of God and as persons for whom Christ died.

Compassion leads Christians to make visible the relatively invisible suffering of many, so that the larger society also may respond to this need. Compassion moves people to anger against that which perpetuates suffering and to defense of defenseless people. Through such actions, Christians respond to the vision of God's future in which blind persons shall see, lame persons shall walk, homeless persons find shelter, and poor persons receive good news. God's community is made manifest over and over again in concrete acts of compassion.

Christians are called to love the "neighbor." The language used to speak about people indicates a great deal about how they are regarded. Some of the terms currently used regarding uprooted peoples—illegal aliens, migrant workers, bag ladies—suggest that these are people radically different from the rest of the human family. Such terms disregard their humanity. As "others" they can then be treated as undeserving of rights, as property or as non-persons who have no valid claim to membership in the human community.

In the order of God's community, however, estranged persons become "neighbors." And because they are neighbors, they are to be loved.

Jesus radically redefined "neighbor" in the story of the Good Samaritan. (Luke 10:25-37) When asked, "Who is my neighbor?", Jesus responded by telling a story about one who "proved neighbor." The burden of proof is upon those who call themselves Christians to define "neighbor" to a suffering world.

Christians are called to seek justice for the poor and power-

less. No theme in the Bible sounds more clearly than the requirement to do justly. (Mic. 6:8) Justice exists when human institutions and relationships mirror God's righteousness. Justice was both the substance of the covenant between God and Israel and the evidence that it was being faithfully kept. Justice is the quality of personal and social interaction that enables each person and the whole community to flourish, to realize their God-given potential, to have the "shalom" of healthy wholeness.

Thus, to keep faith with God is to establish justice among persons. To know God is to do justice and righteousness. (Jer. 22:16) Negatively put, the presence of injustice is a clear indication that God is not known and the covenant with God is not honored. Positively put, whenever and wherever justice is done, it points to the active sovereignty of God in the world.

From a biblical perspective, justice clearly requires partiality to the claim of poor and oppressed persons. Not that poor persons are inherently more worthy or that privileged persons do not also have a claim to justice, rather, the continued situation of poor, powerless, outcast and oppressed persons constitutes an offense to God, an indication of human defiance. In the name of God's righteousness, justice takes the side of the one who is deprived of land and exploited by unfair wages, destitute while others live in luxury, powerless in the face of power-vested interests.

Indeed, God personally defends the defenseless, protecting the weak, advocating the cause of the poor and bringing the mighty down when their positions of power are abused. Justice aims at the establishment of human community in which no person will be victimized, the claims of all will be heard and dealt with fairly, the rights of all will be upheld.

For Christians, justice is an imperative because God is just and wills justice for the world.

Chapter Two:
People Seeking
Refuge

"Refuge" is a word rich in meaning in the Old Testament. It referred most specifically to the six cities which had been set aside to shelter those individuals who had accidentally killed someone, protecting them from the pursuing avengers. (Num. 35:6-15) Some usages can be traced back to the language of warfare such as the "secure height" and the "strong rock." (Judg. 6:2; 1 Sam. 13:6; Isa. 2:19) Hence "refuge" came to describe God as the "rock," a "fortress." (Deut. 33:27; 2 Sam. 22:3; Jer. 16:19)

The Book of Psalms is especially rich in references to God as a refuge. (Ps. 46; 62:1-8; 71:1-8; 91:1-10)

One event in the life of David was recalled by the Hebrew people in their times of trouble. David hid in a cave from the pursuing Saul. (1 Sam. 23:19-24) Two psalms are ascribed to David as having come from that experience, Psalms 57 and 142.

Meditate on Psalm 57:1:

"Be merciful to me, O God, be merciful to me, for in thee my soul takes refuge; in the shadow of thy wings I will take refuge, till the storms of destruction pass by."

Imagine hiding in the cave, recalling some experience when in great fear you were seeking a place of refuge.

Imagine that the Early Warning System has signaled that a nuclear missile is expected to hit your community or city. Is this the feeling of what it is like to seek refuge desperately?

CONFRONTING UPROOTEDNESS

The furnace is on the blink. The house is ice cold in mid-December. What a time for this to happen! A thoughtful neighbor offers refuge, a warm room in which to work. It's troublesome to pick up books, papers, typewriter and move. I am disoriented and it takes a while before my thought processes begin working again. Suddenly it hits me! I am chafing at such a minor dislocation, as I write about millions of persons whose lives have been completely torn up by the roots. I get the message!

The world is now witnessing the greatest wave of refugees in modern times. The numbers of those forced to leave home and country is hard to estimate. In this century so far, perhaps more than one-quarter billion have fled their countries. In the last three years an average of 2,000 to 3,000 new refugees a day have sought asylum outside their homeland. The United Nations High Commissioner for Refugees (UNHCR) estimates that in 1980 there were more than 12.5 million refugees worldwide. However, international relief workers and other experts report between 16 and 17 million refugees for that year.

All sorts of tags are placed on these persons—refugees, displaced persons, expellees, exiles, asylum seekers, aliens, entrants, detainees. The tag is crucial in determining their destiny. But they are individual persons, not too different from anyone else. Christians can attempt to penetrate the welter of statistics by placing themselves in the situation of a few of the world's refugees.

REFUGEES—WHO ARE THEY?

Southeast Asia

Amid shelling, rocket fire and burning horizons, a woman lay in a Saigon hospital bed. Loan Vo Le was alone, coughing, suffering from asthma. All around her people were running away. She prayed for the storm of terror to end and for the strength to breathe and break through the enclosing fire. It was the night of April 29, 1975.

"I sneaked out at four o'clock in the morning despite the danger and the curfew," said Loan. She had left her husband Phuoc Le, her three daughters and her young son at home. Loan was a former American Field Service exchange student in upstate New York, a trained nurse and interpreter. Phuoc had served in the Vietnamese Army Corps of Engineers. Neither had had problems getting U.S. travel documents, but they were already too late for the emergency air lift.

"I went to my sister who lived by the harbor," Loan recalled. "On the armed forces radio we heard 'White Christmas' which was the signal that the U.S. fleet was waiting to pick us up. She told me that everyone had to pay $200 to get out of Saigon by boat. But we only had $20. So she took the boatman into her home because he had to hide during the day to make it look like he was not planning to leave. In payment he gave her six free

15

passages on his boat. So Phuoc, our three daughters, my one-year-old son and I set out to meet the U.S. fleet.''

The Le family's escape took them to the U.S. naval station in the Philippines, to Guam, to Camp Pendleton in California, and finally to Hawaii, where they arrived July 13, 1975. Their son died two days after they left Vietnam of a stomach infection. There they began to make their new home. Loan thinks often of Vietnam and wants to go back, but realizes that it is impossible. "If Vietnam were a free country, I would like to go back. I miss my family so much. But we couldn't stay. I feel like a Vietnamese American," she says, pausing, "But inside I'm still Vietnamese."[1]

In the years since the collapse of U.S. power in Southeast Asia (1975-1981), some 1.3 million Southeast Asian refugees have fled to other countries. Over three-quarters of these persons have been resettled. The United States admitted more than 515,000 and Canada more than 70,000. Many others have been settled in other parts of the world. "Boat people" from Vietnam have continued to arrive in camps in Southeast Asia, especially in Hong Kong, Malaysia, Indonesia and the Philippines. Though camp population is declining, many thousands still await sponsors and new homes around the world.

The situation for the "land people," refugees who fled over land, remains turbulent. Some 290,000 refugees from Laos and Kampuchea (Cambodia) were in camps in Thailand toward the end of 1980, while another 278,000 Khmer refugees were encamped in the area along the Thai-Kampuchea border. Furthermore, an estimated 200,000 Thai citizens displaced by the influx of Kampucheans have moved farther inland. All this adds up to more than three-quarters of a million displaced persons in the area.

Refugee camps can be the first step to saving lives. Often they must begin from nothing. Within a week of the announcement that Kampucheans would be allowed temporary sanctuary in Thailand, the Sa Kaeo holding center was opened. Three days later this muddy plot of land was home to 30,000 people. Relief workers battled the flood, primitive medical facilities, shortages of clean water, difficulties feeding so many hungry people and the overcrowding. For a time, the average daily death toll was 40.[2]

While the life-threatening crisis has been contained, long-range solutions for Southeast Asia's multitudes of evicted and homeless persons remain elusive. Unless a political solution can be found, the tide of refugees is likely to continue, making the whole region unstable and presenting a massive aid and resettlement problem.

Afghanistan

Sometimes they travel by camel. Some are able to come by donkey cart. The most desperate even walk if they have no other choice. Each week several thousand refugees pour into Pakistan from Afghanistan.

By the end of 1980, the number had grown to over 2 million with no sign of the flow abating. Since 1978, civil war has raged between Muslim guerrillas and the Soviet-backed central government in Kabul. Some observers estimate that nearly a half million Afghans have died during the conflict. By the end of 1980, nearly one of every 10 Afghans was a refugee.

The Afghan refugees in Pakistan are scattered in tent villages of 200-500 persons. Most are in the North West Frontier Province, a beautiful but desolate area, where the biting winds blast down through the snow covered Khyber Pass. Less than 10 percent of those in the camps are men; almost all of the men are more than 40 years old. Most men have returned to Afghanistan to fight. "We take turns in fighting. Some of us rest with our families, while others cross into Afghanistan to make jihad (holy war) against the Russians," says Rahmad Jan, a former agricultural inspector. "Over there, Russian planes destroyed everything with their bombs. Our homes. Our fields. We came here to seek shelter with our women and children. We came with nothing. Just the clothes we are wearing. Now we must live like nomads."[3]

Shah Zarina says she could be 10 years old but doesn't know for sure. She pulls her black chadar (shawl) closer around her and shifts her 18-month-old sister to a more comfortable position on her hips. Shah Zarina arrived in Kachigarhi camp with her mother, her grandmother and four younger brothers and sisters. Her older brother, Ahmed Shah, who escorted them to Pakistan, returned to Afghanistan to fight. They had left their ancestral village in Jalalabad province after their father, who had joined the fighting against the new government, was killed.

The family was fairly well off in Afghanistan and managed to bring along some gold ornaments, a couple of wrist watches and a few goats. Through the first winter they huddled under two blankets issued by the Pakistani authorities in a tent they shared with three other families. The family received four rupees, around 40 cents, per person per day to buy food.

Now the ornaments are all gone—sold to buy food, clothes and other urgent necessities. The wrist watches, the blankets and all but two of the goats are gone, too. One of the younger children died some months ago. The other three are constantly sick. The bitter winter cold causes bronchitis and fever. The intense heat of summer causes malaria, dysentery and dehydration.

Like many refugees, this is a group of people who just want to go home. Most Afghans do not want to be resettled. The Pakistani government, which has registered and sheltered them, also wants them to return home and is doing little to resettle them. When the trickle of refugees turned into a tide, the government asked for outside help. Now international and voluntary relief agencies are doing their best to provide food, shelter and basic health care. Plans are also underway for primary schools and vocational training. This refugee situation may be long-term requiring permanent settlement in Pakistan.

Meanwhile, there is a growing sense of isolation and despair among the refugees who feel that in the world with so many pressing problems, theirs is in danger of being forgotten.[4]

Central Europe

As out of Vietnam there have come the "boat people," so out of Central Europe there come the "car people." Their bizarre assortment of vehicles lines the courtyard of the Traiskirchen barracks, about a 30-minute drive from Vienna. The barracks might be taken for a used car lot, except that each vehicle bears Eastern European license plates.

Traiskirchen is Austria's principal refugee reception center. Men, women and children wander among the weathered brick buildings. Roughly 90 percent of these East European refugees are in their 20s and 30s. Some have young families.

A high proportion of them are East Europeans, notably from Czechoslovakia, Poland, Hungary and Romania. They escape during vacation seasons and travel as tourists, making their way to Western Europe. In 1979, more than 5,000 refugees from 35 different nations passed through Traiskirchen, many on their way to countries in Western Europe and North America. In late 1981, thousands of Polish refugees fled their homeland.

Austria is also a first transit point for Jews leaving the Soviet

Union. The Jewish people had been displaced, without a home-land, for more than 18 centuries until modern Israel came into being. It was Jews from Eastern Europe who first immigrated to the place that became the nation of Israel. They continue to leave Eastern Europe and the Soviet Union in great numbers, going to Israel, or wherever they believe they can live without persecution. In 1979 about 52,000 emigrated. An estimated 19,000 went to Israel. Most of the rest settled in the United States; a small percentage went to Australia, Canada, New Zealand and Western Europe. Emigration was more difficult in 1980, following the Soviet move into Afghanistan and U.S. counter measures.

Masha (not her real name) is a young Jewish woman who emigrated to the United States from the Soviet Union in the early 1970s. She tells this story:

"My father was a famous poet in Moscow. He's not a political poet. You don't have to write something which is clearly, strictly opposed to the government. But everything that is really alive, everything that is really talented is opposed by the government.

"My parents emigrated for political reasons. Once he was called in by the secret police and they asked him where he took the books he read and who gave him these books. He didn't want to answer them. He thought that it would be better for us to leave than for him to go to prison again. Under Stalin's time he was in prison and in exile in Siberia. He is really sick and he is 50 years old. He thought that he wouldn't be able to endure it. Another prison and another such experience would just kill him. It was a very hard decision.

"I really don't know what I want to do in the future. Prob-ably I would like to live in America. I hardly think it will be possible to return. I'd like to go sometimes, but just as a tourist, to see my friends. I don't think I will ever be permitted to go there."[5]

Palestinians and Lebanon

The Rev. Aude Rentisi, minister of the Anglican Evangelical Church and Deputy Mayor of Ramallah on the West Bank of Israel, remembers "the Disaster" as though it happened yester-day:

"On July 10, 1948, the Israelis took over my home town Lydda. I remember it was a Sunday. You know, when you are a child things stick with you, you never forget. I remember vividly. It was two o'clock in the afternoon. I saw a man I knew walking past our street with a cane with his handkerchief on top of it. I asked, 'What is he doing?' You know as children we have many games, but never do I remember seeing a man carrying a stick with a white handkerchief on it. 'The Israelis have come, and we are hoping that they won't shoot at us.' Soon the Israelis came and asked us to leave. The British had done the same thing in 1936 to give the soldiers time to search the homes, then leave. We thought this was a repeat.

"So we decided to go to St. George's Church, which my ancestors had served as priests, one of the most ancient churches in the area. But soon the soldiers asked us to proceed to the market place to the end of town. We were led in a narrow lane that led to the mountains. The soldiers searched everyone; we had to give up all our valuables. A young man was shot in front of us because he refused to give up his money. Before we got out of Lydda, we found ourselves with no food and no water for about two weeks. Then we had to walk three days across the mountains to come here to Ramallah.

"One hundred thousand people were evicted from Lydda in one day; 4,000 died from starvation and exhaustion. In Ramallah we stayed at first under trees. Then we found refuge in a Quaker school, four families to a room. Then the Red Cross gave us tents and that was the beginning of the refugee camp.

"Then the United Nations comes and asks Israel to go back because according to the Partition Plan about 30 percent of Palestine was to be given to the Jews. In 1948, the Israelis took 77 percent of Palestine and left us with the West Bank and Gaza Strip—23 percent. Since 1967, they have occupied even that 23 percent.

"Each year the Palestinian problem is being discussed in the UN and decisions taken that Israel should withdraw. I don't understand. Is might right or is right might?"[6]

The oldest unresolved refugee problem in the world is in the Middle East. Refugees from Palestine left their homes over 30 years ago. Today there are some 1.8 million Palestinian refugees living in and out of refugee camps in East Jordan, the Gaza Strip, the West Bank, Lebanon and Syria. Thirty years ago, the UN Relief and Works Agency (UNRWA) began temporary services for the three-quarters of a million

Palestinians displaced by war with Israel. Since UNRWA's beginning, 105 countries have supported its work, but the agency is finding it more and more difficult to obtain funds for its ongoing task of providing relief services, health services, education and training.

Palestinian refugees, according to UN definition, are "persons or descendants of persons whose normal residence was Palestine for a minimum of two years preceding the Arab-Israeli conflict in 1948 and who, as a result of that conflict, lost both their home and their livelihood." Now a generation has grown up in the camps and temporary housing, which has led the United Nations to recognize the "permanent" nature of the crisis.

The instability created by the Palestinian-Israeli conflict has spread into the surrounding region, especially Lebanon. It has ignited conflict between Christian and Muslim groups, and between factions within the Christian and Muslim communities. Countless lives have been lost and property destroyed. In June 1980, the United Nations reported 400,000 in Lebanon as "internally displaced." An American church administrator for the Middle East expressed it this way:

"Lebanon is like a person wounded in the deadly crossfire of battle. As the lifeblood drains from the nation, those with the capacity to bring healing continue to fight each other, oblivious to the critical need of the people caught among the guns. Will the fighting stop in time to save the wounded? Nothing less than the survival of the nation is at stake!"[7]

East Africa

Marian Ahmed lives with another family in a dome shaped hut made of reeds, branches, mud and cardboard. The neatly swept interior contains only a straw mat, a pot and a can filled with grain rations for the next 10 days.

"We have not got enough food," says Marian, who fled Ethiopia for Somalia last spring. "We never get supplies regularly. Either we have too much sugar, or no wheat, or we get oil and nothing else. We never get meat."

At Dam refugee camp in northwestern Somalia, Noora Hassan tells of fleeing the Ogaden to Somalia with her four children because of Ethiopian attacks. "Our homes were destroyed by tanks and planes," she says. "My husband is still fighting there, but we can't go back. It is too dangerous and there is no food."[8]

The nearly dry river bed dividing the camp serves as a wash area for the women and an open sewer. Children splash and roll about in ankle-deep puddles. The rains that temporarily quenched the region's drought also brought mosquitoes carrying malaria. The land around lies ravaged and parched. Parties of refugee women have to wander up to 12 miles to gather firewood. Even with fuel, there is little to cook. Despite international aid, refugees here barely receive half their recommended food needs.

Somali government officials are dismayed by the West's comparative lack of response to their plight. "Compared to Southeast Asians," notes one government minister, "we are being treated like dogs in a gutter. You throw us some scraps occasionally just to keep us quiet and ease your conscience."

Some 90 percent of the refugees in Somalia are women and children. The men are either fighting with the liberation movements in Ethiopia or tending their few remaining cattle, camels and goats back in the disputed Ogaden region. The refugees in Somalia are in danger of becoming the outcasts of East Africa. The Ogaden is presently administered by Ethiopia, but has been inhabited by ethnic Somalis for centuries.

The plight of Somalia's refugees is but one piece of the refugee crisis that grips Africa. With more than 6.3 million refugees and internally displaced persons reported in 1980, Africa is the continent with the largest refugee population. Forced population movements because of human conflict and natural disaster are increasing in this part of the world. The majority of the continent's more than 40 countries are themselves impoverished and often unstable.

Unlike Southeast Asia or Eastern Europe, resettlement outside the continent has not been a solution for most of Africa's refugees. Some observers say this is because refugees from Africa are not welcome in other places. They seek asylum in neighboring countries in the hope that one day they will be able to return to their homelands. Meanwhile, they live in destitution in camps such as those in Somalia or migrate to urban areas, as have tens of thousands of Ethiopians into Sudan. They rely on government, international or voluntary agency relief for basic survival.

Ideally, economic development programs could prevent much of today's tragic refugee flows, often at a fraction of the cost of providing emergency relief. In one part of Ethiopia, for

22

instance, relief agencies are spending more than $10 million in famine relief, whereas pumping $1 million into water construction projects would have offset drought across much of the entire area. Political upheavals and war force huge expenditures on relief to the homeless, shatter the development process, and erode stability still further.

Southern Africa

Southern Africa presents a pattern quite distinctive from that of the refugee situation in the rest of Africa. Southern Africa provides one of the most successful cases of voluntary repatriation, the return of refugees to their homeland, during the past decade. The negotiated settlement of hostilities in Zimbabwe in 1979 brought an end to bitter fighting which had lasted nearly 15 years and driven many from their homes. Peace made possible the return of over one million people who had been displaced within Zimbabwe or had left the country during the years of fighting. Many came back to find their homes and fields destroyed and their livestock missing, but friends and relatives have helped them reestablish themselves. The government, with assistance from international and voluntary agencies, has begun the formidable task of providing education, health and employment opportunities for a new beginning.

Along with this success story, southern Africa presents a grim example of people becoming refugees because of racism. Mass arrests and the fear of torture by the racist South African government have forced some 60,000 people to flee Namibia (formerly Southwest Africa) and make their way to camps in neighboring Angola. One such person is Rauna Nambinga, a young nurse, who told of beatings and solitary confinement by the South African police after she was arrested at the hospital where she worked.

"The most terrible day I remember was when I was taken to a small room. There were many pictures of dead people on the wall. They told me one was my brother, Usko Nambinga, so I must show them which one. Because I would not comply I was again beaten. From there I was taken to a room where there were snakes and I was told that if I was not going to start telling the truth I was going to be bitten. I was in great panic."

Later she was tortured by electric shocks, prolonged hanging and severe beatings. A military doctor told her that she had serious head and kidney injuries and burst ear drums. When she was released after months of solitary confinement, she fled Namibia, afraid for her life.[9]

South Africa has displaced thousands of Namibians to create a "security zone" along the 1,000-mile border with Angola. Churches, schools, clinics and homes were destroyed. While the UN Security Council has condemned South Africa's illegal control of the area which had been a UN trust territory, negotiations have failed to bring peace.

Equally grim is the fate of nearly two million blacks within South Africa who have been uprooted from their homes and dumped in barren, crowded "bantustans."

All of the country's 20 million blacks are technically attached to one of the 10 tribal homelands where they theoretically do what they can't do in South Africa—vote, own property and enter any restaurant they wish. Though South Africa has declared four of these to be "independent homelands," none has received recognition by any nation besides South Africa.

Ciskei is one such homeland that was granted "independence" on Dec. 4, 1981. The Rev. Ray Magida teaches the Ciskei people to grow vegetables to improve nutrition standards. He says: "It is the back yard where South Africa throws what it regards as rubbish—the black people it does not want."

For the 666,000 Xhosha people who live in Ciskei, only 106,000 have jobs either in Ciskei or in South Africa proper. In urban areas one child in 10 dies of malnutrition before the age of one. In rural areas, one child in four dies of malnutrition before reaching the age of one.

Many of the Ciskei "citizens" were simply loaded onto government trucks in white South Africa and dumped in open country. They had run afoul of one of the apartheid schemes designed to keep down the number of blacks living in the 86 percent of the country officially designated as belonging to the 4.5 million white South Africans. This white population is only 16.4 percent of the persons living in South Africa.

Latin America and the Caribbean

Refugee statistics for Latin America are deceptively small—only 239,000 officially reported for 1980. Such figures do not reveal the depth of the suffering experienced by many forced to flee the dictatorships that characterize many nations in Latin America.

Well known to many is the exodus that has taken place from

Cuba since the victory of Fidel Castro in 1959. The total now numbers more than one million, out of a total population of 9.5 million. People from Haiti have arrived on U.S. shores, approximately 12,400 in 1980. The number is now declining, although many still arrive. As Central America erupts, conservative estimates are that some 150,000 refugees from El Salvador and some 80,000 from Guatemala have fled to neighboring countries. Some have come to the United States.

Little is said in the news media regarding the thousands who have fled the torture of right-wing dictatorships in South America. The United States has not been as receptive to these refugees as Canada and nations of Western Europe have been. Yet the crackdown by military governments in South America in the 1970s led some 250,000 to leave Argentina; an estimated 80,000 Chileans have fled their country, and an undetermined number have sought refuge outside their home countries of Brazil, Bolivia, Paraguay and Uruguay.

The story that many of these uprooted tell is one not so much of mass deprivation and suffering as of selective cruelty and torture. One such person is Adriana, a Chilean woman whose son remains in prison. For reasons still unknown to her, Adriana (not her real name) was permitted to leave Chile for the United States. "She is less an immigrant than an exile. She is less a pilgrim than an expatriate. She does not speak of the American dream but the Chilean nightmare with American ghosts," says Thomas Bentz of her in his book *New Immigrants: Portraits in Passage.*

Her story begins in September 1975, after a U.S.-backed military coup had overthrown the elected Chilean government of Salvador Allende.

"We lived in a house where we had a clear view of the street. Crowds were uncommon because no one in Chile was allowed to gather a group in public. People were picked up and disappeared at random. Terror and fear were everywhere. So when I saw a group gathering in the street, I went out to investigate. Rumors had spread around the neighborhood that someone was going to get picked up. Outside on the street corner, I overheard the police say that they were looking for someone. I listened to the description. It was my son.

"I went back to the house. Juan was there. So were six of his student friends who had come to defend him when they heard he was in danger of arrest. Soon forty or fifty men in civilian clothes arrived, surrounded the house, and pointed guns at us. They were members of DINA, the only group allowed to carry guns in Chile. They were the national investigation force, trained by the CIA of the United States.

"All eight of us were arrested and blindfolded. My son was accused of being a delinquent, of belonging to a socialist political group. It was damp and cold, and I was stripped of my heavy jersey and overcoat so that I could feel the chill . . . .

"We were going to La Casa de Tortura—the House of Torture . . . When we arrived, though we could not see, we knew where we were. I heard the screams of the young man who had come to our house earlier that day to warn us . . . .

"Finally they took me to a room in the prison that looked like an old kitchen . . . There was no furniture, no bed and no blanket. All I had were the thin clothes I wore . . . .

"Suddenly my door opened and someone came in, struck me, grabbed my hair, and dragged me over to the next cell where they were keeping my son. They had his hands tied behind him, and they sat me down in front of him. They began punching me with fists like hammers in my temples and asking over and over, 'Is this your son?' But I didn't say anything. Finally Juan said, 'Yes, I am.' Then they took me back to my cell and left."

Adriana's story continues. In 1976, she was given the chance to leave Chile, and she took it.

"I came to the United States not because I wanted to come, but because my family and friends thought that if I did my son wouldn't have to suffer anymore. I chose this country because at the time other countries would have taken longer. I came here to get away from the intimidation, but I'm beginning to think that it's hopeless . . . .

"If the United States wanted to, it could get my son out right away because it was this country, through the CIA, that got all of us into trouble in the first place. They are the ones who trained the secret police and backed the brutal regime that now has my son imprisoned.

"You know I have no power here, no power to vote or to affect the system. If the U.S. does not allow me into its politics, then the U.S. should not become involved in the politics of my country. Years ago, your banks gave millions of dollars to Chile, money with which the junta bought all the arms and everything else it needed to terrorize the people."[10]

26

In this tumultuous world much has happened since the writing of the above accounts. Look for updates on the situations described, as well as any new refugee crises which have arisen since early 1983, when this book was published.

WHY DO THEY FLEE?

"It is the refugee who reveals to us the defective society in which we live," says Melaku Kifle, refugee secretary of the All Africa Conference of Churches. Kifle says the people who become refugees are mirrors through whose suffering everyone can see the injustices, the oppression, and maltreatment of the powerless by the powerful.

Through this brief summary of the contemporary refugee situation there is seen a wide variety of underlying factors which take ordinary people and turn them into refugees. There are the "push factors" such as war, disaster, famine, political upheaval, oppression and violence. There are also "pull factors" such as the search for survival, freedom, self-determination, and economic stability.

The personal examples given so far in this chapter indicate numerous underlying "push" and "pull" factors. Note the similarities, dissimilarities and interrelationships among the various cases.

As this monumental catastrophe is considered major themes and trends begin to emerge.

Refugees are casualties of a world in conflict. Since 1945, at least 75 wars have wounded the peoples of the world. Undoubtedly, a relationship exists between the world's warring and the number of refugees. People uprooted by war are the tragic evidence of the inability of nations and peoples to manage their hungers, their politics, their religions in a manner that takes due consideration of other human beings.

Most refugees are people for whom home is no longer a secure place because of political unrest in the form of persecution or oppression, or upheaval in the form of war, terrorism or revolution. Those political structures that violate fundamental human rights and force people to leave their homes are all too often pawns in the struggle of the world's superpowers.

The brunt of today's refugee burden is borne by Third World countries. Today's refugee populations are concentrated most heavily in the world of poor nations. "The character of the world refugee problem has changed dramatically over the years," comments Dale de Haan, former UNHCR Deputy Commissioner who is now Church World Service Immigration and Refugee Program Director. "The focus has turned to the Third World where we are getting waves of fleeing populations rather than individuals."[11]

Many Western countries have made substantial efforts in refugee work. At the same time, more and more countries in the less developed world are not only the source of the largest refugee movements, but are also host to the majority of refugees and displaced persons. These Third World countries pay a high price in terms of domestic instability and deferred development hopes. Frequently remarkable instances of generosity to the homeless and uprooted are found in the middle of desperate poverty. The appeal from these countries for a reasonable degree of burden-sharing, both at the regional and international levels, has generally met with lukewarm and inadequate response from the more economically developed nations. Consequently international agencies that carry responsibility for lifesaving ministries among refugees usually have woefully inadequate resources.

Population increases have not been accompanied by more equitable sharing of the earth's limited resources. The world has become more densely populated with half again as many people today as there were in 1960. Large numbers of people are inevitably caught in the conflict over control of limited resources. Rivalry over land has intensified. Empty habitable land areas which used to absorb large numbers of refugees and new settlers have been virtually exhausted. As poverty holds more people than ever in its grip, tensions erupt into violence.

National borders created during the colonial era are a source of ongoing contention. The period of colonization by European nations in the 19th century was the beginning of many of today's problems. This is particularly evident in Africa, which is now producing half the world's refugees and displaced persons. The arbitrary boundaries drawn by the colonial powers left a legacy of discontent by dividing ethnic groups and tribes, placing them in different nations. This chopping up of territory became significant in the turmoil of newly independent countries seeking to establish national identities. Along with this the ongoing struggle against colonialism, particularly in southern

Africa, forces many who are politically active to flee to avoid imprisonment or death.

Women and children form the largest part of the world's refugee population. It is no accident that the majority of the personal examples given in the earlier part of this chapter are women. Not that men are any less the victims of world conflict. However, they often remain behind, engaged in fighting, thrown into prison, trying to keep the last vestige of the family's claim upon a precious piece of land. Meanwhile refugee camps are crowded with fatherless families. Women must serve as both mother and father and must carry the double burden of nurturing children while learning the skills needed for survival. All too often refugee policies and programs have been addressed to men, ignoring the much more critical needs of women whether in camps or in places of resettlement.[12]

It goes without saying that the upheaval of the refugee experience has lifelong traumatic impact upon the lives of children. The family often is split up. The new pattern of social organization is unfamiliar. Health hazards are enormous. Children must skip the carefree days of childhood and join prematurely in the grim battle for survival. The price that is paid in robbing the nations' and the world's future of stable, educated youth is beyond comprehension.[13]

The increasingly small world neighborhood has yet to learn how to be neighborly. The worldwide communication network enables people, even in the most remote areas, to know what is happening in the rest of the world. Refugee movements become "news" and are widely reported. The media powerfully influence the attitudes that people take toward refugees, and when these attitudes are shared by whole populations the effect on the well-being of refugees can be profound. Along with this, the comparative ease of modern transportation enables refugees to be somewhere else overnight. Many refugees in Canada are known as "plane people" since the principal point of entry into the country is the airport. This may lead North Americans to think all refugees are seeking entrance to their countries, overlooking the fact that the greatest number still trudge by foot or cart to the nearest border or other haven of safety, hoping against hope that the day will come when they can return to their own land.

This accelerating movement of people and ideas across the globe has not been accompanied by a willingness to accept the pluralism which characterizes an increasingly interdependent world. Heightened racial, ethnic, social, political and economic tensions not only create refugees but also slam the door in their faces. To live as global citizens means accepting with thanksgiving and expectancy the gifts that are brought by the rich variety of the world's peoples.

HOW TO DEFINE "REFUGEE"?

Unusual as it may seem, there is no comprehensive definition recognized by all countries as to who is a refugee. The closest thing to it is the United Nations Conventions and Protocol Relating to the Status of Refugees, ratified in whole or in part by only 78 of the more than 150 countries in the United Nations. The conventions define a refugee as a person who "owing to well-founded fear of being persecuted for reasons of race, religion, nationality, membership of a particular social group, or political opinions, is outside the country of his (her) nationality and is unable, owing to such fear, is unwilling to avoid himself (herself) of the protection of that country.

This technical question of who is and who is not a refugee has enormous significance for the displaced people themselves. It may well determine whether they will be received in the country to which they flee and the degree of support and protection they will receive. Those governing the countries from which people flee often dispute the validity of refugees' claims to politically-based asylum calling them "guerrilla fighters," "terrorists," "dissidents" or simply "voluntary migrants." Countries on the receiving end, in turn, may dispute the claims of refugee status, giving to the displaced people such titles as "illegal aliens," in order to avoid the obligation a nation bears when large numbers of homeless people descend upon it.

Of course, a basic distinction must be made between "refugees" and "immigrants." "Immigrants" usually leave their homelands voluntarily. They are motivated not by fear of persecution, but by the desire for change. They may have a possibility of employment or be prompted by family or other personal reasons. Once at their destinations, immigrants generally have some personal resources or receive support from family members or friends.

Refugees, on the other hand, are usually forced to leave their country with few if any personal possessions. Refugees require, at least temporarily, food, medical care and shelter. The distinction between refugees and immigrants, however, is not always clear-cut. In some cases, motives may be mixed. It becomes difficult to separate the fear of political persecution from the desire to leave grinding poverty linked to a political system.

People who flee their homeland without any "right" to enter another country live in a legal limbo. They apply only to people who are outside the boundaries of their own nation; internally displaced people are not helped by them. International conscience is still in the process of developing laws that will place primary value on the lives of all those who are forcibly uprooted in the global community.

Increasingly the attempt to improve the lot of refugees has focused on establishing the principle of asylum to ensure that refugees are not repelled and sent back to the countries from which they have fled.

Many countries of the world are becoming increasingly restrictive in admitting asylum-seekers by introducing stricter border controls and visa requirements. Now no country escapes the risk of becoming a "country of first asylum," as uprooted people arrive by plane, boat, car or on foot. Growing unemployment, overriding concerns for national security, fear of racial conflicts and fear of overpopulation are all used to keep refugees out. While the basic right of "non-refoulement," not expelling refugees without due process of law, is a commitment made by nations that ratify the UN Convention and Protocol, numerous governments have violated this fundamental right and that is happening on a rapidly growing scale.

The UN instruments were designed with the individual refugee in mind. But nowhere do the documents anticipate the mass exodus that in recent years has dramatically swelled the number of refugees in the world. Consequently, many of today's refugees are not dealt with by international policy. Among them are the problems attending the struggles for independence and national identity and the huge movements that are a mixture of political, economic, social and ethnic factors. The community of nations has yet to learn how to deal with the victims of conditions which cause entire populations to flee.

WHAT ARE THE ALTERNATIVES FOR REFUGEES?

Because refugees are usually the victims of circumstances

beyond their control, they often have no personal choice in what will happen in their lives. Yet, from this point of view the international community sees three basic alternatives: voluntary repatriation, settlement in the country of first asylum, and resettlement in a third country.

Voluntary repatriation, that is, refugees returning home of their own free will, is ideal both for the refugees themselves and for the countries and agencies that work with them. Logistically and psychologically it is the easiest solution. Politically, it is usually the most difficult. It requires that the crisis that drove people from their homeland be resolved. Further, returned refugees will need material support until they can reestablish their lives.

Despite the difficulties, numerous successful cases of voluntary repatriation have occurred during the past decade. The case of Zimbabwe has already been cited. The most massive recent repatriation involved the return of more than 10 million Bengalis to the new nation of Bangladesh in 1972. These refugees had fled to India during the war of independence and the subsequent Indo-Pakistani War. Caring for them during their exile was a monumental task. When the war ended, authorities of the Indian and Bangladeshi governments worked with the UNHCR in organizing the refugees' return. In less than four months, the 10 million persons had gone home and the refugee camps were closed.

Lessons learned in Bangladesh were put to good use throughout the '70s with smaller scale repatriation efforts in Angola, Burma, Guinea-Bissau, Mozambique and more recently in Nicaragua.

Permanent settlement in the country of first asylum is a poor second to voluntary repatriation, but in many cases it is the only practical alternative. The welcome that a country of first asylum extends to refugees depends on a complex set of considerations:

a) the strength of the receiving country's economy;

b) the compatibility of the refugees with the local population;

c) the speed and generosity of the international community's response to the need for humanitarian assistance;

d) the political stability of the host government; and,

e) the foreign policy stance of that government toward the conflict that forced persons to become refugees.

Often countries of first asylum face a huge struggle to meet the basic needs of their own citizens, so that supporting additional displaced people represents an awesome burden. The government of Somalia has welcomed the Somali refugees from Ethiopia with open arms, both because of ethnic ties and because Somalia has long laid claim to the Ogaden region from which the refugees have come. But, the need for humanitarian assistance is far beyond what that nation itself can provide.

In a racially heterogeneous society, an influx of refugees may be seen as upsetting a delicate balance. In 1979, Malaysian authorities refused for a time to give even temporary asylum to ethnic Chinese fleeing Vietnam because of Malaysia's own internal struggle between native Malaysians and immigrant Chinese. The presence of refugees may raise even further the level of tension between neighboring countries.

On the other hand, cultural traditions may also play a part in attitudes toward refugees. Several African nations, such as Sudan and Tanzania, have set aside land for the permanent settlement of refugees who have come from neighboring states. In the words of Tanzanian President Julius Nyerere, "the refugees of Africa are primarily an African problem, and an African responsibility."

For many refugees, the costly and time-consuming process of resettlement in a third country is the only viable alternative. Some persons flee with no expectation of returning, such as Jewish emigres from the Soviet Union. Others leave with the fond hope that one day they will return, but come to realize that resettlement is the only option. The largest and most dramatic instance of third-country resettlement in the past decade is the ongoing case of Southeast Asian "boat people" and their counterparts who have fled Kampuchea, Laos and Vietnam by land.

The process is painfully slow and terribly expensive, as international and voluntary agency staff members interview each person to determine whether s/he qualifies for resettlement. Requirements are complicated for each country agreeing to provide a limited number of opportunities for resettlement of refugees. The needs for third-country resettlement of refugees continues to be as pressing as ever. Resettlement, however, must not be viewed as "the answer" to the refugee crisis, but only as a last resort.

If these three basic solutions do not work, the remaining

alternative is grim indeed. For some persons, flight from war or persecution will turn or has turned into lifetimes, even generations, of exile. The most prominent such case is the Palestinians, most of whom were displaced over 30 years ago. They are still awaiting a solution to "the Palestinian problem." The bitter experience of prolonged uprootedness deeply scars those persons who live through it. Their suffering is a reproach to the international system that has been unable or unwilling to provide a viable alternative for their survival.

WHAT ARE THE LONG-TERM PROSPECTS?

No one following refugee issues in recent years is very optimistic. The forces that form refugee crises are, if anything, gathering strength—population growth, competition for land and resources, unequal distribution of wealth, disputes over international boundaries.

Nonetheless, the forming of an international consensus on acceptable norms of behavior of nations moves ahead with excruciating slowness. Although many kinds of imperialism persist in the world, the old system of Western colonial domination is definitely on the way out. The international community is beginning to develop stronger forms of moral and political pressure to dissuade governments from forcing their own internal problems onto the world community by expelling entire groups of people from their homes.

These issues will take years, even decades, to resolve. The United Nations continues to work steadily to extend international protection to refugees and to provide material assistance from public sources for persons in need. It deserves far greater support than it receives at present. Private voluntary organizations, especially the churches, play a key role both in short-term emergency relief and in the more long-range response of refugee resettlement and development programs. They need much greater financial backing.

Ultimately the refugee crisis is but one aspect of a disordered world. A statement on "The Churches and the World Refugee Crisis," adopted by the Central Committee of the World Council of Churches in August 1981, includes the following:

"The indispensable counterpart to giving refugees emergency and even longer-term help is to understand why the recipients have become refugees and then attempt to take corrective action. Only in this way can the problem be understood in its totality and progress made toward solving it at its roots . . .

"Churches everywhere should state and show their refusal to accept the chaos and injustice of the world as it is, and express their solidarity with all the refugees who have become its victims. Translated into action, this expression of solidarity means for the churches a much fuller participation in the search for global justice."

Chapter Three:
Giving and Withholding Refuge

No love was lost between the people of Israel and the Moabites. Never would Israel forget how the Moabites had refused their ancestors permission to pass through the Moabites' territory on the way to the promised land. (Judg. 11:17) Nor would the Israelites forget how the Moabite king, Balak, alarmed when the Israelites camped in his vicinity, sent for Balaam to curse them. (Num. 22-24) For this hostile attitude, the Israelites were commanded to exclude the Moabites from their midst and to remain cold and indifferent toward them forever. (Deut. 23:3-6; Neh. 13:1-3)

In the face of that "closed door" policy, it's refreshing to hear the story of the blessing which one Moabite refugee, Ruth, brought to Israel and eventually to the whole world. How did Ruth become connected with the people of Israel? (Ruth 1:1-5) What brought Ruth and her mother-in-law Naomi back to the land of Judah? (Ruth 1:6-14) What kind of commitment did she make in leaving her own land and coming to Judah? (Ruth 1:15-18) Note the tenderness of the relationship between Ruth and Boaz. (Ruth 2:8-13) Savor the happy ending of the story. (Ruth 4:9-17)

Why is this story in the Old Testament? What do Christians have to learn from Ruth? (Matt. 1:5,6,16)

Now, think of people who have arrived recently in your community as refugees. What brought them? What kind of commitment did it take for them to come? What kinds of personal relationships can individuals and churches have with them? What contribution do persons seeking refuge have to make to their new communities? To their new nations? How does all this affect attitudes about the policies that the nation should have regarding refugees?

"Give me your tired, your poor,
Your huddled masses yearning to breathe free,
The wretched refuse of your teaming shore,
Send these, the homeless, tempest-tossed to me:
I lift my lamp beside the golden door!"

—Quotation from *The New Colossus*, by Emma Lazarus, inscribed on the base of the Statue of Liberty

"Our biggest trouble is that unfortunate statue in New York harbor. France gave us this statue in 1856, when we were young and foolish. France has no such inviting statue at its border, nor does any other nation. Other nations know better. We Americans still suffer from an adolescent's illusion of unlimited power to do good."

—Garrett Hardin, biologist and human ecologist, quoted in the *Sentinel Star*, Orlando, Fla.

"Canada has a long and distinguished record in assisting refugee movements. However, an incisive and systematic evaluation of Canada's refugee program over the years reveals an interesting observation. Economic considerations have played a paramount role in the numbers and occupational affiliations of refugees granted asylum in Canada. At times it appeared that the economic benefits were considered equally, or even more important than the humanitarian sentiments."

—Constantine Passaris, associate professor of economics, University of New Brunswick

"Despite all the problems in our cities today, despite all the burdens that our communities are bearing with unemployment, inflation, housing and taxes, you should recall that the record of history is clear: Whenever we have helped others to come here and build a new life, . . . there have always been those who would close the golden door, but afterwards we have always been able to say, 'By helping these people, we have helped ourselves.' Our role as a beacon of freedom in a darkening world is too precious a part of our tradition, too central to our strength as a free people, to allow it to weaken even in the hardest times. If we ever determine that the Statue of Liberty has become obsolete, we may find that we have become obsolete also."

—Victor Palmieri, former U.S. Coordinator for Refugee Affairs

How do these quotations reflect past U.S. and Canadian national policy? Current U.S. and Canadian policy? What should U.S. and Canadian policies be? If you could reword the quotation on the base of the Statue of Liberty, how would you express what national policy should be toward the world's uprooted people?

WHO GIVES REFUGE?

"Fellow immigrants!" began President Franklin D. Roosevelt in an address to the Daughters of the American Revolution. Offsprings of tempestuous times, these women had become, in but a few generations, the rock-hard guardians of U. S. isolationism. In the roar of the 1920s and the following decade of depression, the golden statue of New York harbor saw the door nearly close to the world's "huddled masses."

Today, as then, North Americans face the danger of forgetting who they are and from where they have come. Not that they have closed "the golden door." Both the United States and Canada, consistent with strong traditions of concern for human rights and people in need, have responded to the world's refugees with resettlement of hundreds of thousands of refugees and contribution of millions of dollars to international refugee aid. Yet, lest North Americans think they are alone in undertaking this task, consider the following statistics:

RESETTLEMENT TOTALS OF RECEIVING COUNTRIES, 1975-80[1]
(Ranked by ratio of refugees to population)

NATION	SIX-YEAR TOTAL OF REFUGEES	POPULATION (millions)	RATIO OF REFUGEES TO POPULATION AS OF 1980
Israel	105,700	3.9	1:37
Malaysia	102,100	14.0	1:137
Canada	84,100	24.0	1:285
Australia	51,200	14.6	1:285
U.S.	677,000	222.5	1:329
Hong Kong	9,400	4.8	1:511
Tanzania	26,000	18.6	1:715
France	72,000	53.6	1:744
New Zealand	4,100	3.2	1:781
Switzerland	7,500	6.3	1:840

Of course, if the above chart were prepared on the basis of ratio of refugees to available land or to economic strength, a number of other nations would surpass the record of both the United States and Canada.

As for the record of giving for official international aid to refugees, the United States and Canada are low on the list:

1980 CONTRIBUTIONS TO INTERNATIONAL REFUGEE AID AGENCIES[2]
(Ranked by contribution per capita)

NATION	CONTRIBUTION ($ million, U.S./equiv.)	POPULATION (millions)	CONTRIBUTION PER CAPITA
Sweden	33.0	8.3	3.98
Norway	15.2	4.1	3.71
United Arab Emirates	1.9	.8	2.43
Denmark	12.2	5.1	2.39
Kuwait	2.5	1.3	1.91
Switzerland	9.7	6.3	1.53
Netherlands	18.8	14.1	1.33
Qatar	.3	.2	1.30
Saudi Arabia	10.6	8.2	1.29
Liechtenstien	.04	.03	1.23
Australia	13.6	14.6	.93
U.S.	199.4	222.5	.90
Canada	18.0	24.0	.75
Japan	81.1	116.8	.69

Both the United States and Canada resettled refugees and contributed to international aid for refugees. But their peoples should not assume they are bearing the burden alone, or even carrying a proportionate amount of it. Many other countries are just as deeply involved.

No one can deny that the United States and Canada play pivotal roles. At pledging conferences of the United Nations, other countries look to these two nations as standard setters. Today, more than ever, this leadership role is important both on humanitarian grounds and on the grounds of doing a fair share toward stability in a terribly unstable world.

WHAT IS OUR HISTORY?

"Once I thought to write a history
of the immigrants in America;
then I discovered that the immigrants
are American history."
  —Oscar Handlin[3]

The first immigrants to the New World came not to empty expanses, but to a land peopled by Native Americans. These many tribes for immeasurable thousands of years possessed a cherished identity. They had lived in a close but free bond with the two billion acres of land on this continent. These Native Americans extended a welcome to the strangers from Europe. The survival of North America's first immigrants depended to a great extent on the hospitality of these Native Peoples.

Yet, U.S. and Canadian histories reveal alternating attitudes of hospitality and hostility toward receiving people in search of refuge.

The 19th century saw the floodgates opened to all who would come to the new nations. From 1819, when the U.S. government first began counting immigrants, until 1920, some 34 million came to its shores, primarily from Great Britain, Northern and Western Europe. They were driven by war, famine and poverty. They followed a promise of prosperity. They came to push white frontiers westward and to help turn the heavy machines of industrializing North America. Not included in these statistics were the men, women and children brought in chains from Africa to provide slave labor. This refusal to recognize the entry of Africans into this country is only one expression of prejudices which have marked U.S. and Canadian histories. In the 1870's a large anti-Chinese movement grew up, and African immigrants were prohibited long into the 20th century. In the midst of the flood of immigrants, some "Yankee natives" felt threatened. In response to prejudice against Irish Catholic immigrants, one Manhattan newspaper editor wrote, "The floodgates are open. The dam is washed away. The sewer is choked. The scum of immigration is viscerating upon our shore."

In one of the darkest pages in U.S. refugee history, Congress in 1939 declined to pass a special bill which would have permitted the immigration of 20,000 children fleeing Nazi Germany, although they already had U.S. sponsors. Martin Die, a member of Congress at the time, said, "We must ignore the tears of sobbing sentimentalists and internationalists. And we must permanently close, lock, and bar the gates of our country to new immigration waves and then throw the key away."

World War II, for reasons good and not so good, led to the beginnings of change in U.S. immigration policies. In the wake of World War II, refugee camps filled with people displaced by war. Private voluntary agencies, including churches, pressed for admission of such persons to the United States. Thus the United States enacted its first official refugee policy, the Displaced Persons Act of 1948. This act permitted 400,000 persons forced from their homelands by World War II to enter the United States. Certain conditions had to be met including the provision that voluntary agencies must agree to meet the full costs of resettlement.

Canada's first "refugee" population was loyalists fleeing the new nation of the United States for British North America. Canada was not yet born as a nation, but the loyalists chose to escape the new U.S. political system and remain true to the crown.

Russian Mennonites were the first to seek asylum in Canada after confederation. In 1874, 2,000 Mennonites left Russia seeking religious liberty. The decision to accept the refugees was based on what the new persons offered the pioneer nation.

Canada's refugee laws have always been quite selective. Only the fittest and most qualified, those most able to foster the nation's economic growth, were allowed to enter. Immigrants who are not seeking asylum from politically oppressive situations are asked to prove they have means of financial support, usually a job, waiting in Canada, and that there are no Canadians available for that work.

The collapse of the Saigon government in 1975 brought a sudden migration of people from Southeast Asia. Many sought refuge in the United States and Canada. Reactions were mixed, especially in the United States which had had a long military involvement in Vietnam. Some people in both nations were afraid of the impact that so many refugees might have on the nation's communities. Nevertheless voluntary agencies, especially the churches, rose to the occasion.

By 1981 over 515,000 Southeast Asian refugees had been effectively resettled in the United States. The U.S. Congress designed the Indochina Refugee Assistance Program to provide cash, medical assistance and social services to Southeast Asian refugees through federal agreements with state and local governments and private voluntary agencies. In many respects, it has been the "finest hour" in the history of U.S. response to the world's refugees.

Nevertheless, other persons fleeing authoritarian governments in Spain, Chili and Brazil were not even considered for political refugee status.

For the first time in Canada's history there was no trace of economic considerations or any degree of self-interest in its response to the Southeast Asian refugees. A substantial number of refugees were airlifted from the temporary refugee camps and brought to Canada on special Canadian Armed Forces flights. Constantine Passaris, an associate professor of economics in New Brunswick, described Canadian response this way:

"Special mention should also be made of the outpouring of public enthusiasm for the refugee sponsorship program which allowed individual Canadians, voluntary associations and church groups to respond and participate in the costs and responsibility of resettling many thousands of refugees.

"Recently Canada has welcomed the 10,000th refugee from the Southeast Asian Refugee Camp in Hong Kong. The 60,000th refugee from all Southeast Asia arrived in Montreal in December 1980."

It can well be said that this was also Canada's "finest hour" in its history of refugee response.

WHERE ARE WE NOW?

U.S. Response

The turbulent world and the pressure of concerns from within led to a realization that U.S. response to the refugee situation had been haphazard, arbitrary and often discriminatory. President Jimmy Carter in 1978 appointed a select commission to review and recommend changes in immigration and refugee legislation, with special emphasis to be given to undocumented workers and illegal aliens. Even before the commission had completed its report, Congress approved the Refugee Act of 1980, the first comprehensive U.S. legislation dealing with refugees.

The Refugee Act of 1980 was viewed by many as a critical turning point in U.S. immigration history. Intended to stand as irrefutable evidence of U.S. humanitarian and democratic ideals and concerns, it was hoped to also be flexible enough to meet the rapidly shifting needs.

Everything seemed to be in place for a coherent and comprehensive refugee policy. However, just a month after the new law was enacted, it was sorely tested. Suddenly the United States found itself no longer simply dealing with refugees at arm's length, sorting through those in camps on the other side of the world and choosing those who met carefully designed criteria. Rather it was flooded with people from two island nations just south of the tip of Florida, Cuba and Haiti. Almost overnight, the United States came to know what many Third World nations have experienced in the past decade, becoming a country of first asylum, the first available and appropriate country in which refugees seek haven or asylum in their flight from oppression.

The United States did not face the rapidly changing refugee situation alone. Although the flow of refugees was not as great in Canada, Canada too faced new refugee and immigration problems, problems not allowed for in Canadian immigration law. One of the first groups of people seeking first asylum from what they considered to be a politically unbearable situation for many, and, imprisonment were U.S. citizens. During the Vietnam war young men left the United States for Canada rather than fight in a war in which they did not believe. Canada received the young men, giving them asylum.

Canada's Response

Canada has accepted more refugees, per capita, than any other of the "developed" nations since World War II. Canada's 24 million people have received more than 350,000 homeless or displaced persons. Looking behind the numbers, church and humanitarian groups contend that Canada tends to express "cautious kindness."

Canada tends to reject those who have fled right-wing regimes, though overall their record on this is better than that of the United States. For example, in May 1981, the Canadian Ministry of Employment and Immigration announced plans to admit refugees from El Salvador and Guatemala.

Because of Canada's location, refugees do not cross its

borders in great numbers as often happens in other nations. Most refugees who enter Canada are selected by immigration officials in overseas refugee camps. Relatively few choose Canada as a country of first asylum.

In contrast to the United States where resettlement is almost entirely the task of private voluntary organizations, Canada's policy provided for the certain number of officially government-sponsored refugees in addition to those sponsored by private organizations. This enables the churches to increase the number of refugees resettled in Canada and balance out government policies. This is done by sponsoring refugees from areas of need neglected by the government and by taking "difficult case" refugees who otherwise might be rejected.

Raul Vicenzio, a director of Amnesty International's refugee section in Canada, summarizes the Canadian situation. "What is required is a change of attitude. The majority of people who have come here have come because Canada needs them. I think in at least some cases, refugees should be able to come to Canada because they need Canada."

Canada's most current immigration legislation contains provisions for refugees. Passed in 1976, the legislation makes refugees a separate admissable class. Until then Canada had relied almost exclusively on ad hoc administrative procedures in order to admit and resettle refugees. However, Passaris, economics professor, says, "Even in this act the criteria used for the selection of refugees demonstrate a pronounced emphasis on economic factors such as the ability of refugees to assimilate in the economic structure and fabric of this country."

The Canadian law has also been criticized for leaving the way open for discrimination. Canadian church leaders have said the legislation would "Ignore our responsibilities to share living space with as many as possible and would grant the privilege to enter this country only to a designated number each year if they serve as means to our own ends." The statement was signed by leaders of the Anglican Church of Canada, the Canadian Conference of Catholic Bishops, the Lutheran Council of Canada and the United Church of Canada.

The statement continued to say the immigration debate "reveals that we are tending to look upon newcomers to this land with selfishness and fear. It also shows that these attitudes are widespread."

Specific problems with the bill include refugees' lack of opportunity to defend themselves in person during the review of their application.

First asylum is not an easy issue to resolve. How many refugees and immigrants can Canada admit? What should be the procedure for hearing refugee claims? Who should decide? Should government policy distinguish between refugees fleeing oppressive governments and physical reprisals and persons fleeing poverty and starvation brought on by government policy?

First Asylum

It is especially important for U.S. and Canadian citizens to look carefully at the issues raised by the growing numbers of people seeking "first asylum" in their land.

Among the continuing difficult cases are the "new boat people," Haitians in search of a chance for survival. Haitians have been coming to North American shores for several years. In 1974 threats to deport 800 Haitian refugees in Canada set off a huge controversy that continues to rock the Canadian immigration and refugee law. The officials refusing to allow the Haitians to stay claimed that the Haitians if deported did not "face reprisals" and if "we gave the kind of special treatment they want to everyone who came because he was displeased with the economic or political situation of his own country, we would have them coming by the millions."

For the Haitians this was to become a familiar official line. Haitians have come in increasing numbers at peril to their lives to U.S. shores. Within a matter of a few months in early 1980, more than 125,000 Cubans arrived in Florida in the "freedom flotilla." During the same time Haitians began arriving in increasing numbers at great risk to their lives. Uncertain how to respond, the administration had earlier announced that Cubans and Haitians known to the U.S. Immigration and Naturalization Service as of June 19, 1980, would be made eligible for status as "Cuban/Haitian Entrant (Status pending)."

What ensued was chaos. Affected communities, especially in Southern Florida, shouldered enormous burdens; voluntary agencies were hampered by government confusion. By the end of 1980, all but 5,000 of the Cuban entrants somehow had been resettled. However, almost all of the Haitians were either in detention camps or living in fear of being arrested and deported.

Through many appeals and court decisions Haitians in the United States waited in hot overcrowded detention centers, which were in reality prisons. They waited for the U.S. court system to decide their fate. Their choice was to return to Haiti where they faced beatings, extortion and death or stay in the detention camps. It wasn't until late 1982 that the court process began to release some of the Haitians. Their future was still uncertain.

At the root of the problem was the question on what do these refugees base their claim to asylum in the United States and Canada? Neither nation accepts economic oppression as a basis for granting asylum. To be considered a political refugee the fleeing persons must prove they face certain political reprisal and personal danger. One Canadian court heard the testimony of a Haitian man that he had been tortured by electric shocks, but he could not prove his claim and refugee status was denied.

The United States immigration system has done no better. Given the U.S. history of racially prejudiced immigration policies, the fact that the Haitians are black undoubtedly made it easier for the U.S. Immigration and Naturalization Services to develop and begin implementing a plan for their rapid deportation which a federal court later described as "prejudicial and discriminatory." An INS official testified that never before had INS processed a comparable number of asylum claims in such a short period of time. Immigration defense attorneys were frequently scheduled to appear in 15 different cases at five different locations at the same time. They were allowed only about 20 minutes to prepare each case.

The key to the issue of first asylum in the United States rests, as it does in Canada, on the same central question as it does for many other refugees—Are these immigrants to be considered refugees from political oppression? If so, asylum may be granted. If not, the asylum seeker is to be deported.

People who work for refugee resettlement see that another issue evolves out of this question of political oppression. In both the United States and Canada there are charges of serious violation of basic civil rights in the hearing and deciding of refugee status claims. It seems that the foreign policy stances taken by governments are often more crucial in the decision-making than the actual substance of the refugee claims.

Canadian Law

Canada's 1976 law provides for three admissable classes:

— the family class, which includes sponsored dependents including parents of any age sponsored by Canadian citizens;

— refugees;

— any applicants, comprising immigrants selected on the basis of selection criteria.

Under the section on refugees the bill makes provision for establishment by regulation of special selection standards for refugees. The government is allowed to respond to special situations where admission on humanitarian grounds is warranted. The bill also outlines provisions dealing with individual civil rights for refugees who "show up" in Canada, seeking asylum, without going through Canada's lengthy selection process for refugees in camps overseas. Two that are important are:

— All whose admission is denied have the right to a full and impartial immigration inquiry.

— A special class of trained officials known as "adjudicators" will weigh the evidence presented before deciding on a person's admissibility in accordance with the law.

U.S. Law

The Refugee Act of 1980 provided for:

1) redefining the term "refugee" to correspond with the UN Protocol definition, thereby doing away with the previous narrow definition of a refugee as "a person fleeing communism";

2) removing refugee applications from other immigration ceilings, providing an annual ceiling of 50,000 refugee admissions;

3) empowering the President, after consultation with Congress, to admit additional refugees in case of "an unforeseen emergency" in a fixed number "justified by grave humanitarian concerns or the national interest";

4) establishing an Office of U.S. Coordinator for Refugee Affairs, and also an Office of Refugee Resettlement;

5) authorizing $200 million annually for services to refugees, providing the first sure financing on which voluntary organizations could count;

6) authorizing the Attorney General to establish asylum procedures for persons seeking refugee status after arrival in the United States. Few foresaw that the limitation in this section would become the Achilles heel of the act.

The clear anti-Castro stance of the United States made the decision to allow the Cubans to stay more clear-cut. More than 125,000 Cubans arrived on Florida's shores in the "freedom flotilla" just a few months after the new U.S. law was put into effect. Most of these arrivals were accepted as political refugees and granted asylum.

But the United States has consistently given aid to the repressive, though non-Communist, government of Haiti.

Even the clear-cut cases are no longer so clear-cut in Immigration and Naturalization Services policy. Refugees from Afghanistan were refused political asylum in 1982. Yet, the United States government has been clearly against the Soviet intervention in Afghanistan.

Ethiopian refugees, after a long and arduous battle, were granted political asylum during the same time period that the Afghanistanis were denied asylum. Most of these refugees had already settled into life in the United States and were self-supporting, or were receiving aid from one another.

In 1979, the United States adopted an "extended voluntary departure" policy with regard to Nicaraguans fleeing the civil war in that country. The policy provided "temporary refuge" and continued until the fall of 1980 when hostilities ceased in Nicaragua. A new wave of persons fleeing civil war in Central America then swept into the United States. This time they were from El Salvador.

The United Nations High Commissioner declared that such Salvadorans should qualify for refugee status. The United States, tied politically and through the military to the existing regime in El Salvador, refuses to grant Salvadorans the same status as had been granted to Nicaraguans, proceeding to deport those who were apprehended. Salvadorans are considered "economic" refugees, as are the Haitians and Afghanistanis. The government of El Salvador, as with the government of Haiti, has long received U.S. foreign aid dollars. A recent decision in Los Angeles federal court found that Salvadorans had not been informed of their right to apply for asylum.

Against such a background the Select Commission on Immigration and Refugee Policy, appointed in 1978, presented its report to the President and Congress in March 1981. The commission summarized its recommendations as "closing the back door" to persons whose immigration was undocumented or illegal and "opening the front door a little more to accommodate legal migrations in the interests of this country." With regard to opening the front door, the commission supported the provisions of the Refugee Act of 1980, already in place.

The commission did attempt to deal with such as those of Cuban and Haitian refugees. The commission recommended establishment of an inter-agency body to open and manage federal processing centers. This was intended to streamline the admission/refusal process. There is a danger that the streamlining will result in a loss of due process of law for applicants. Each mass asylum applicant would have to prove his or her refugee claim individually. The U.S. Refugee Coordinator could develop "group profiles" to determine the legitimacy of asylum claims.

Meanwhile, the newly-elected Reagan administration picked up the initiative on the "refugee crisis." The administration authorized the Coast Guard to intercept and turn back Haitian refugee boats on the high seas, returning those who seek asylum in the United States to their homeland without a chance of hearing or petition for legal status. The needs of Salvador refugees have not been addressed and in July 1982 apprehension and deportation continued.

The "new austerity" of U.S. Immigration and Refugee Policy became more evident as months passed. A U.S. Department of State directive on refugee resettlement for 1982 contained a 35 percent reduction in refugee admissions, with 90 percent of those admitted having to come from Communist regimes. It included cutbacks in social service programs available for refugees and increased monitoring by the government.

Church and voluntary agencies engaged in refugee resettlement faced the difficult task of meeting increasing needs with reduced resources and growing demands of government.

Trends in the Reagan administration immigration policies seem clear. Federal control of resettlement of refugees has increased. At the same time, federal money for refugee resettlement is being decreased. There is a lessening of the numbers of refugees allowed to resettle. However, a new emphasis has been placed on the reuniting of families, a long-upheld priority in immigration policy among persons working directly with immigrants and refugees.

New legislation debated in 1982 and being acted upon as this study was being prepared would severely limit the civil rights for those seeking first asylum in the United States. The Simpson-Mazzoli bill, as it was named after its sponsors, would allow the staff of the Immigration and Naturalization Services to act as judges and juries in determining the fate of refugees seeking first asylum. Opponents of the bill see it as the beginning of basic denial to right of hearing, petition and counsel. The current Canadian law sets up similar special officials to hear and decide cases, without review of the court system. Those in favor of the bill herald it as a streamlining of immigration process and argue that as non-citizens the refugees are not entitled to the same rights as citizens. The issue of a right to individual hearings is crucial to the future and lives of literally thousands of men, women and children who come seeking refuge.

Much will have happened since this section was written. Look for updates on developments since the fall of 1982.

WHAT SHOULD OUR POLICIES BE?

The events of the past few years have thrust upon North Americans some profound questions. What should they do about all the uprooted persons coming to their nations? Should they take in all the refugees? Should all refugees be turned away? If North Americans take in some and not others, how will the choices be made? Which ones? How many? If some people are helped, will others come in even larger numbers? What do national ideals and Christian faith require of North American citizens in such a time as this?

The issues of immigration and refugee policy are complex and controversial. Government decisions are made on the basis of a number of considerations: the nature of society, and the rights and privileges of citizens and non-citizens, the needs of the poor already within North American borders and the use of limited resources.

The real problem lies at the point where national self-image and self-interest conflict. Wanting to help uprooted persons is part of values which have been a source of national pride. Fairness and morally upright conduct in both public and private life is fundamental in both U.S. and Canadian national identities. North Americans see themselves as basically a generous and compassionate people. They want to do what is right. But, North Americans often see "doing what is right" as a threat to their lifestyles. This may not be true at all. In helping others, many agree, North Americans usually help themselves.

At this point religious roots greatly affect answers. Review the first chapter before proceeding to think about what national policies should be.

Several major religious groups have adopted statements on national policy regarding immigration and refugees.[4] While they vary in emphasis, the major thrust of the statements is remarkably consistent. Here are the principal themes:

1. *Immigration laws should be equitable, fair and consistent in respecting the rights of all people.* One suggested measure of fairness calls for an admissions policy that is non-discriminatory with respect to the elements of human equality contained in the Universal Declaration of Human Rights: race, color, sex, language, religion, political or other opinion, national or social origin, property, birth or other status.

2. *Numerical limits on immigration should recognize national interests while also acknowledging an obligation to the world community.* Nations should extend aid and opportunity to immigrants not only because they may contribute to national interests and profit, but simply because people are in need.

Some have expressed concern that admitting refugees will lead to North American nations becoming overpopulated. As a matter of fact, the United States and Canada are among the nations with the least population in ratio to land area. If they can't receive the world's uprooted, who can? Another dimension exists as well. Concern has been expressed over the steady decline in population growth in the United States and Canada. The declining birthrate has produced more and more people at or near retirement age and fewer people approaching working age. The select commission's report said younger immigrants could help even out this imbalance, strengthen the potential labor force and increase the taxpaying population in relation to the retired population.

3. *Immigration should not be based exclusively on an applicant's national origin.* The National Council of Churches of Christ policy statement "opposes as unjust the system of restrictive national-origin quotas." Current United States' law is susceptible to discrimination based on quantitative immigration ceilings by country. The current U.S. limit of 20,000 immigrants per country was not intended to discriminate, but

has resulted in long backlogs that have a discriminatory effect. The limits could be abolished and replaced with other provisions for selecting immigrants. Within three years, say some authorities, this would eliminate the huge waiting list afflicting many Third World immigrants.

4. *Enforcement and administration of immigration law should provide non-citizens with the same basic guarantees of fairness which are provided to citizens.* The U.S. legal process assures the constitutional right to a fair trial—including a presumption of innocence, a neutral judge or jury, the right to confront witnesses and the assistance of an attorney. Refugees and immigrants are at present generally denied these rights.

Instead, the U.S. Immigration and Naturalization Service exercises virtually unchecked authority in making the determination of an alien's status. Hearings are not conducted by independent judges but by INS employees, which tends to bias decisions in favor of the agency, according to the U.S. Commission on Civil Rights. Congress could change this by spelling out the rights of non-citizens and, more importantly, by structuring the enforcement agency (INS) so that it will respect these rights. One important right which should be included is judicial review of INS decisions.

5. *Any preference system should respect the need of other countries for their most talented and trained people.* Many nations have complained that U.S. and Canadian immigration policy favors the wealthy and talented who have the skills required for entry. A "brain drain" of professions from Third World nations is thereby encouraged. If criteria are dependent on education skills, there will be little opportunity for anyone other than the privileged to enter. The opportunity to emigrate should be extended as well to the poor and underprivileged.

6. *Since immigration law is federal law, only the federal government should enforce it.* Some state and local authorities have attempted to enforce immigration law or impose restrictions on immigrants or refugees. At times local police have jailed people whom they suspected of being undocumented immigrants but who were in fact citizens or legal residents. Far more often, social services have been denied to those who indeed qualify.

7. *Family relations should be respected, with the reuniting of families as high priority.* This is a principle which has been clearly stated in UN standards regarding immigrants. Yet there

has been a proposal for a 10-year waiting period for spouses and children to join illegal aliens now living in the United States. This kind of proposal actually promotes the breaking apart of families. For the United States to adopt such a policy would be a giant step backward.

8. *The United States and Canada must abide by the principle of non-refoulement, not forcibly returning those who seek asylum.* When Thailand and Malaysia threatened to push boatloads of refugees back on the high seas during the mass exodus from Vietnam, many U.S. and Canadian citizens became incensed at such inhuman treatment. Yet now the United States has announced that the Coast Guard is to intercept, search and turn back vessels suspected of transporting "illegal aliens." In this and other efforts the United States is guilty of violating one principle agreed on in consenting to the UN Protocol and made into law in the Refugee Act of 1980. The determination of asylum status is a lengthy process and certainly cannot be done by the boatload on the high seas. Likewise, the development of detention centers has become punitive and violates the basic human rights of those who have come seeking asylum.

9. *The United States and Canada should provide generous support to the homeless of the world.* Support should come both in the form of humanitarian aid to nations experiencing a large influx of refugees and in assistance to voluntary agencies undertaking refugee resettlement. The United States and Canada are far down the list in contributions per capita to international refugee aid agencies. Certainly these nations can do better. The United States has a proud tradition of relying heavily on private voluntary agencies to undertake the task of refugee resettlement. Yet federal governments, in their zeal to trim budgets, should not assume that voluntary agencies, or state, provincial and local governments, can pick up the slack in refugee programs. Such programs are being carried out on behalf of the whole nation.

10. *Global power should be used to support economic and social justice in other nations and in U.S. and Canadian relationships to those nations.* The causes of migration cannot be ignored, even if they are beyond the scope of immigration law. War, oppression and economic injustice in other countries become immediate concerns when victimized persons seek refuge. Such conditions can often be attributed to national

policies and practices. Facing up to economic, development and military involvements abroad is basic to stemming the tide of refugees. The NCCC statement concludes by renewing its commitment to work for just and equitable relations between the United States and other nations "which would contribute to the well-being of all peoples and hence to the elimination of the causes of involuntary emigration."

Other national policy issues will be presented in the next two chapters. Examine the policy statements adopted by individual denominations and by national councils of churches. What other policy principles are stated? What would you add or subtract?

WHAT CAN THE CHURCHES DO?—
GIVE REFUGE

Three major channels are available for refugee aid. One is the international route. Among the variety of international agencies, the chief source of assistance is the office of the UN High Commissioner for Refugees (UNHCR). Founded in 1951, this worldwide agency with representation in over 80 countries protects refugees, promotes durable solutions to their plight and provides emergency assistance as solutions are sought.

A second channel for refugee assistance is bilateral government aid, operating independently of the international agencies. Both the United States and Canada have programs of this nature, related especially to refugee resettlement.

The third major route for response is through voluntary agencies, popularly referred to as "volags." In cooperation with UN agencies and national governments, volags have taken on a large share of the responsibility for refugee relief and resettlement. Their financial resources are modest compared to government funds, but their contribution cannot be measured simply in dollars. Their promptness, flexibility and neutrality enable them to fill critical gaps during emergency situations. The logistical and operational expertise built up by volags over years of refugee relief work surpasses that of many governmental agencies. Volags take up where governments leave off, helping refugees build new lives, providing moral support, orientation, practical advice and friendship. As one commentator has put it, the volags "stand between the individual refugee and the impersonal machinery of government. They have excelled in treating the refugee as a person."[5]

Among the volags with a remarkable record in refugee relief and resettlement are the churches. They have acted from the local to the national level, denominationally and ecumenically. Many of the churches in the United States work together in this ministry through the Immigration and Refugee Program of Church World Service (CWS). Through its member denominations, CWS helped resettle 33,655 refugees in all 50 states in 1980. The total refugee resettlement for CWS since its program began in 1946 is over 300,000. In Canada, churches work together in refugee relief, resettlement and advocacy through the Inter-Church Committee for Refugees. But this is only a small part of the resettlement efforts made by volags. CWS and many denominational agencies work to resettle most refugees internationally.

The constituent denominations, through their refugee resettlement office, generate sponsorship in local congregations, prepare congregations for arrival of refugee families, and provide resources and guidance as the congregations undertake the task.

The local congregation is where the action is. That's where people dedicated to the refugee ministry take responsibility for welcoming the refugees upon arrival, helping provide housing and furnishings, helping provided the basic necessities, helping the breadwinner secure employment, introducing the newcomers to the community, arranging for language and skills training program and enrolling children in school. Most of all, the love and friendship of a caring community is offered these newcomers.

The human drama experienced as thousands of congregations have taken on this ministry deserves much greater length than afforded here. A few vignettes may give a bit of the flavor.

From Laos to Virginia

On Thursday, July 31, 1980, at 9:56 p.m., the Saleum family—Hieng, Boundhome, Deng, Manivanh and Bounthanon—four days out of a refugee camp in Thailand, arrived into the arms of Three Chopt Church. The 20 or so Three Chopt Welcomers were allowed to go to the receiving area of the airport. These were anxious moments as it appeared that no

Laotians were getting off the plane. Finally the five came out of the plane and towards the door where the welcomers were waiting. Pheng, one of the interpreters, began to scream, in Laotian, so the others didn't know what she was screaming. She interpreted herself quickly: "I know her! I know her!"

"The tears of joy began to flow for them, for us, for reunions, for refugees, for freedom, for America, for peace, for God's love for us, for our love for each other, for the ability to hug and to smile to communicate that love without words. When there was not a Saleum available to hug, we hugged each other. They were here. The Saleum family was in Richmond, Va., U.S.A."

—from the newsletter of Three Chopt Presbyterian Church, Richmond, Va.

Being There

"In the morning, Kathleen Ptolemy heard a father threatened to kill his child in Canada rather than see him deported to his homeland to face persecution and possible death. In the afternoon she had a telephone call from a panic-stricken family in Chile whose young son had fled to the United States having learned he would have to wait one month for a visa from the Canadian Embassy before leaving Chile. He's now behind bars in a Miami detention center, and Ptolemy says it will be at least three years before release.

"Ptolemy is co-ordinator of the Canadian churches' answer to the worldwide refugee crisis."

—Joanne Fairhart Houlden, "What We Can Do from Canada", *The Observer,* United Church of Canada.

Hearing the Word

The congregation of West Ellesmere United in Toronto has discovered a way to include Spanish-speaking refugees in the life of the church. The congregation holds a weekly Bible study class conducted in Spanish. Most of the 20 participants are members of a refugee family from Nicaragua, the Castros. They began to attend West Ellesmere after meeting the Rev. Don McCallum, former minister of the church. McCallum and the Castros began a conversation at a bus stop where they waited together. McCallum's smattering of Spanish and the Castros' meager English didn't keep them from communicating. The Castros came to church the next Sunday and

they and the church have been together ever since.
—*The Observer,* United Church of Canada

Grief and Comfort

Choeun Koet and his wife Saroth planned to escape from Kampuchea, but each time they were unsuccessful until April 11, 1976, almost a year after the Khmer Rouge took over. With two other friends, Choeun and Saroth disappeared into the jungle, heading for Thailand. They reached Thai soil 26 days later.

Choeun was then placed in prison for 30 days. He never learned why. Finally records were found that showed his loyalty to Lon Nol's government. By August, Saroth and he were sent to Illinois. With deep grief they left son and daughter behind, not knowing what had become of them. As Choeun put it, "We had lost our country, our honor, our children— everything. We came with nothing. We had no relatives in Chicago and knew nobody."

In 1978, Saroth was hospitalized for about a month with illness and depression, still grieving over the loss of the children. At the hospital, she and Choeun met Doris Johnson, a social worker and concerned Christian. Doris suggested that Choeun and Saroth visit the Covenant Community Church of Edgewater, near where they lived. This church proved to be a base of emotional support for the lonely couple. Choeun speaks of Covenant Community with the highest regard, as a strong and essential rock in his and his wife's past emotional waste-land. Since then, Choeun and Saroth have steered many other immigrant Kampucheans to the church.

—from *The Other Side,* July 1981

Of course, the refugee resettlement done by local congregations has never been free of problems. There is an unavoidable amount of difficulty for the refugees in coming to a completely new country, learning a new way of life, and dealing with the grief of lost family, friends and homeland. Not everyone who is uprooted is able to put down new roots.

Local congregations also bring their own expectations into a refugee resettlement project. The local church cannot help but hope the refugees will quickly grow to love the family, friends and homeland of their new hosts. But resettlement remains for the most part the only answer for many refugees. Whatever the combination of costs and opportunities, resettlement is a cooperative effort between people having roots and those seeking, in the oldest biblical sense, a place of refuge.

Building on the basic work of local congregations, many creative developments have taken place in refugee resettlement:

—Church World Service has developed a national network of local and state offices, called Ecumenical Refugee Resettlement and Sponsorship Services, which help sponsorship development, identifying local services and employment, language and vocational training, counseling.

—Transit centers have been established in such diverse places as Los Angeles, Brooklyn, New Windsor, Md., and Comer, Ga., to provide an intermediate step as refugees move into life in this country.

—Volunteer language teachers have been recruited to introduce refugees to "basic survival English," usually in space donated by local churches.

—In communities that have experienced increased inter-ethnic tensions, churches together have sponsored meetings to improve communication between refugee groups and various groups in the community.

—Churches have helped persons resettled in their area to market their distinctive arts and crafts.

—Churches have interceded in defense of refugees as they encounter difficulty with a legal system they do not understand.

In numerous other creative ways, churches and individual Christians have worked together to assist refugees as they become a part of the life of their new nation and community.

WHAT CAN THE CHURCHES DO?— ASSIST IN OTHER NATIONS

Whatever their faith or ideology, it is to the churches that many of the world's displaced people will turn in distress. In most countries to which refugees flee, the Christian community is small. Even if it is large numerically, resources may be severely limited. The support of the global Christian community is desperately needed if these partners in Christ are to fulfill their calling to minister to the strangers in their midst.

The World Council of Churches, through its Commission on Inter-Church Aid, Refugee and World Service, has become the major switchboard through which churches around the world assist one another in the overwhelming task of refugee relief and assistance. By far the largest need is in Africa. The Sudan Council of Churches, for example, seeks help in ministering to the 490,000 refugees in that country coming from the neighboring states of Ethiopia, Uganda, Zaire and Chad. Its ministry includes programs of emergency aid, health care, social service and self-help projects.

Similar programs are being undertaken by churches in 16 countries in Africa, four countries in Asia, seven countries in Europe, and 10 countries in Latin America. Also, the Middle East Council of Churches undertakes an extensive program to respond to the many needs of Palestinians.

In some places of great need, virtually no Christian community exists. It then becomes necessary for Christian agencies from abroad to address both immediate relief needs and more long-term development problems.

The Kampuchean Example. Such an approach is represented in the Church World Service program undertaken in Kampuchea. The project aims at stemming the flow of refugees from the devastated land and preparing the way for repatriation for those who fled to nearby Thailand.

Halting starvation and reviving food production meant starting from "below zero," as Kampuchean colleagues put it. After initially concentrating on food shipments and medical relief, CWS switched its emphasis to helping rebuild irrigation systems and improving the health of oxen and water buffalo, the living tools of cultivation and transportation.

Exports were necessary, but the Kampuchean government was reluctant to admit specialists from the United States. So CWS turned to Christian colleagues in Cuba. Through the Christian Council there CWS secured the help of Cuban technicians, a hydrologist to train survey crews to repair war-damaged dikes and canals and a veterinarian to train farmers to vaccinate cattle and treat widespread outbreaks of cattle diseases. The agricultural program, focusing on Kompon Speu province, a hard-hit area near the capital city of Phnom Penh, is taking the war-scarred earth, still riddled with land mines and unexploded shells, and bringing it to life again as this nation struggles to achieve food self-sufficiency. CWS Executive Director Paul McCleary says of the Kampuchean Recovery Program, "it uniquely illustrates the act of churches rising above almost insurmountable obstacles to give witness to that which united us and to affirm the value of the person in the wake of the world's most recent holocaust.''

Through Church World Service and the appropriate denominational agency Christians can secure an update on each church's response to partner Christian agencies abroad who are ministering to refugees and to programs addressing situations which create refugees. What has your congregation done to assist such programs?

WHAT CAN THE CHURCHES DO?— ADDRESS ROOT CAUSES

In this day of uprooted millions, North American nations and churches have an opportunity to express genuine compassion by assisting the world's refugees. Yet who would dare to think that such a response is sufficient in itself? The suffering, the agony, the destruction of human rights and of life itself which have forced this tidal wave of people across national boundaries demands that North Americans acknowledge the larger setting within which their efforts take place. No work of refugee resettlement or assistance is adequate without recognition of the systemic factors that must be challenged.

North Americans' limited efforts must be seen in the context of the larger drama that is taking place and in which they inevitably are actors.

To be sincerely concerned about the world's refugees, then, will lead Christians to examine and address such key issues as violations of human rights, foreign military intervention, support of oppressive regimes, poverty and economic injustice. It will lead churches to encourage and support movements for human rights in all nations, to work for the peaceful resolution of conflicts, to push for economic and social development that meets the genuine needs of people. It will lead congregations not only to keep themselves informed, but also to educate and sensitize the community about those forces which are at work that are disrupting and uprooting the lives of millions.

Roy I. Sano in "Co-working With God to Create a 'Good and Broad Land.' '' said, "We work with refugees . . . because we work with a God who creates livable space. When such space degenerates, this God . . . arouses us to liberate the space from domination, from lesser rulers who are inevitably oppressive, abusive, and illegitimate. This applies to our ideologies, institutions or individuals . . . Amen.''

Photo: United Nations/UNRWA

Palestinian refugee in Baqa'a Emergency Camp.

Chapter Four:
No Land No Refuge

The congregation is in the middle of worship when suddenly someone bursts into the sanctuary, interrupting the service with a tirade about the way rich people are crushing poor people. A scene from the sixties? Guess again! The prophet Amos is at the Jeroboam "church" in Bethel. (Amos 7:10-17) Consider a modern translation of his message:

"Hear this, you who trample upon the needy and bring the poor of the land to an end, saying, 'When will the Festival, a day of rest for workers, be over, that we may sell grain? And the Sabbath, that we may offer wheat for sale, that we may conspire with bankers and rig our scales in order to cheat the poor and maximize profits, that in league with both temple and court we may foreclose on the debts of the poor and take title to their land?'"[1]

Amos spoke the word of God to the Israelites in the eighth century B.C. when their nation was at the height of its territorial expansion and economic prosperity. By taking advantage of its war-torn neighbors, Israel gained control of the major trade routes of the ancient world. Successful foreign expansion gave rise to a powerful merchant and urban class, and to unprecedented affluence. The rich slept on beds of ivory, feasted sumptuously, drank wine from bowls and anointed themselves with the finest oil. (Amos 6:4-6) They were the "notable people of the first of nations." (Amos 6:1) And they celebrated their affluence far removed from the suffering of poor persons on whose backs their wealth had been built.

Farmers with small land holdings were particularly victimized. They were pressed off their land and became landless laborers. They worked land they once owned, for the benefit of absentee landowners. (Amos 5:10-12) Other displaced farmers moved to the urban centers where they were at the mercy of greedy merchants who held monopoly power over the grain market. (Amos 8:4-6) In normal times the merchants merely exploited these displaced persons. In bad times they held life and death power over them.

Amos insists that the spiritual root of all this injustice was idolatry. The temple flourished along with the unjust prosperity of Israel; religious leaders were accomplices in the suffering of poor persons in Israel. Therefore, Amos insists, through their worship the people actually multiply their sins (Amos 4:4) and prepare the way for their own destruction. (Amos 2:6-8, 13-16)

Harsh words! Are there parallels to the present day? What relation is there to the biblical teaching that ultimately it is God who owns the land? (Lev. 25:23-28)

"CUT OFF FROM THE SPIRIT OF THE EARTH"

Many Native American have not adjusted well to relocation in the city. Cash grants from the government induced their move from their centuries-old homes. Tom Begay, who started drinking heavily after he moved to Phoenix, often spent the night weeping. "It wasn't just a matter of getting used to the city life," says the Navajo. "It was the feeling of being cut off from the spirit of the earth. I don't think the folks in Washington can understand that."[2]

Trace land ownership patterns in your family. How do you feel about the land? What did Tom Begay mean when he talked about "the feeling of being cut off from the spirit of the earth"?

To speak of roots is to speak of land. To speak of being uprooted, then, means most literally to speak of being pulled up from the earth. For many of the world's uprooted people, this is exactly what has happened. They have been pulled up from that place where their roots were deep, where they belong. The land had been the source of their livelihood and life for them and their forebears. This is not a phenomenon of the past. Rural poor persons are being uprooted from their land at an accelerating rate around the world and in the North American nations as well.

A 1975 World Bank study indicates that in 83 countries surveyed slightly more than 3 percent of all landholders control nearly 80 percent of all farmland. In comparison, the number of landless or near-landless rural people is growing rapidly. In Latin America, over a third of the rural population must make do with just one percent of the land. In Africa, three-quarters of the people have access to not quite 4 percent of the land. In all nonsocialist developing countries 30 to 60 percent of rural adult males are now without land.

What has brought about this alarming trend? The problem dates back to the period of colonial expansion when Western empires carved out their colonies in Asia, Africa and Latin America. Conquering powers subverted whole nations and cultures, usurping resources to serve the interests of colonizing nations. Traditional patterns of land use were disrupted, and the plantation system came into being.

The plantations produced new crops, not for the well-being of the people, but instead for the markets of the colonizing powers. Sugar, coffee, tea, cotton, tobacco, rubber and banana plantations became the pattern for agriculture in the colonies, using the best agricultural land and uprooting rural peoples who had occupied them. Many of the rural native population lost their land and became tenant farmers, sharecroppers and migrant workers on the plantation. Some were able to keep less desirable pieces of land, usually in the hilly or more arid parts of the country.

But colonialism is dead, isn't it? Politically, it is almost a relic of the past. Its indelible imprint on every society sets the pattern for both land and labor. The postcolonial period is often referred to by Third World nations as the era of neocolonialism. Even after political independence was achieved, economic dependence continued.

Poor countries still depend on export of agricultural products and raw materials to Western nations for the bulk of their foreign exchange earnings. They have found themselves caught in an economic web of selling their basic commodities at a low rate set by the Western countries while buying back manufactured products from Western nations at an increasingly high price. No wonder that their economic situation began to deteriorate rapidly. "In 1900, people in poor countries had a per capita income about one half that of people in rich nations. By 1970 it was about one twentieth of the rich nations measured in 1900 dollars, and one fortieth in 1970 dollars."[3]

The gap between rich and poor countries was widening before inflation was considered. After inflation, which is disproportionate, is considered, the gap is even wider.

The economic dependence of poorer nations has served as an entering wedge for large corporate interests from Western nations. They have moved in force into the lives of the "less developed nations," ideally to assist in their "development,"

63

practically to gain the advantage of cheap land, raw materials and labor and wide open marketing opportunities. In doing so, they have worked hand-in-glove with the landed elite of those countries. Dispossessed of their land, rural poor persons are forced to seek a living in the cities. This rural-urban migration, prompted primarily by landlessness, has become a major social problem in many developing countries. Most of these uprooted families migrate from rural areas into city slums. Housing is poor and overcrowded. The lack of clean water and similar services create health problems and high infant mortality rates.

Such conditions create a political powderkeg. Throughout the Third World, rural people's movements have emerged. The rural poor and dispossessed are demanding a more just and equitable system. They are calling especially for the revision of land use and ownership patterns. All too often such demands are met not merely by indifference but by cruel oppression. The elite minority who control the government secure military assistance from those abroad who find it profitable for the system to remain unchanged. Finally the forces demanding change will wait no longer. Bloody revolution can erupt. The rural poor become the major victims and, again uprooted, flee across national borders seeking refuge. Taking a closer look at specific situations will make the plight of the world's landless clear.

CASE STUDY: THE PHILIPPINES

"One of the first things you must realize," said Mang Juan, a Filipino rural leader, "is that we live in two different worlds. It is as if you live in the world of the birds of the air, and we in that of the fish of the sea. When birds move, they, of course, move faster because they fly. On the other hand, when we fish move, we move relatively slower because we have to swim in an ocean.

"And so it sometime happens that some birds want to do good to us from the height in which they fly. Condescendingly they say, 'Mr. Fish, progress! Move like I do—this way and that—so you could move faster! We fishes, of course, cannot follow because we have to move in this ocean of usury, and tenancy, and other unjust forces.

"Very few of the educated people will come into our world and see the reality of our problems and aspirations from our point of view."[4]

64

The Philippines, an archipelago of 7,000 islands, seven languages and 57 dialects, is the only predominantly Christian nation in Asia. This is the fruit of the era of Spanish occupation, when conquistadors and friars came together, beginning in the 16th centruy, to establish Spanish rule and the Roman Catholic faith. The United States has had a dominant influence in the Philippines following the Spanish-American War in 1898. Some Filipinos speak of their history as "three centuries in a monastery and three generations in Hollywood."

Sharecropping existed in the Philippines even before the Spanish conquest. But the Spanish utilized the system to secure the labor of the indigenous people on the large estates they had assigned to themselves. Now, companies rent sections of these estates. Since local people often have no other means of livelihood they accept whatever contract terms the company is willing to grant. The people stay with the land, not as a matter of law, but of economic necessity.

So today about 55 percent of the entire Philippine farming acreage is used for export crops—sugar, coconuts, bananas, rubber, pineapple, coffee and cocoa. Much of this farming is directly controlled by foreign interests in cooperation with a small number of local elite.

Take, for example, the case of the two large fruit companies, Del Monte and Dole, both owned by Castle and Cooke, Inc. The companies themselves own relatively little land. Yet through complicated joint-venture arrangements with the Filipino National Development Company, they actually control some 18,000 and 9,000 hectares (27,000 and 13,500 acres), respectively.

In response to the successful efforts of their workers in Hawaii to increase wages, these companies have shifted pineapple production to a variety of "underdeveloped" countries, including the Philippines. Wages can be as low as 15 cents an hour. By contracting with owners of large land holdings, the companies themselves supply to the landowners the credit, fertilizers, pesticides and other agricultural needs for the purpose of producing the export crops. These same landowners also do the dirty work of uprooting tenants by eviction, wresting land from farmers and enforcing wages far below an acceptable living standard. In this way the corporations are able to assume a low profile and disclaim responsibility for the oppression of the people in the countryside.

Much of the land now producing products for export was formerly used by these farmers and tenants to produce corn and rice, much of it for local use. The tenants have simply been evicted while the owners of small farms have lost their land through a variety of insidious maneuvers by the large landowners and companies. Often persons whose families have farmed a piece of land for generations have been evicted because they did not have proper titles to the land. According to a recent estimate, 80 percent of the rural labor force—once landholders—are now landless laborers. Many work as tenant farmers on land they once owned.

So, what are the landless to do? One option is to go to the cities. In 12 years (1958-1970) metropolitan Manila grew threefold, from 1.7 to 4.4 million, mainly because of mirgration from the countryside. Experts predict that by the year 2000 it will reach 11.7 million. The "squatter" population, which had been growing at around 14 percent annually, reached over one million in 1970, more than 30 percent of the total urban population.

The conditions in one of the slums of Manila is vividly described by a Filipino church leader: "As we near the area, we see the massive tall buildings of the BLISS project, a government-sponsored tenement program that both gives some hope to the residents of the crude shanties all around it and at the same time mocks them as they realize that only a favored few can enjoy it. All the rest of the area looks like an unruly sea of huts and hovels, put together with cardboard boxes, pieces of metal and anything else that can be propped together for shelter.

"People are everywhere. Children run around constantly. A long line, mostly children, stand waiting to pump water out of the public 'poso.' More than half of the adults are without any work whatsoever, and the rest are underemployed."[5]

But there is another option for the rural poor, both farmers with small land holdings and the landless people: organize for struggle. That is happening in the Philippines, no matter how great the opposition. In the 1960s, the Free Farmers' Movement had been a national rallying point, but was crushed down with the declaration of Martial Law in 1972. At present, despite the repression from the government, local people's organizations are sprouting up again. A key word through the long history of rural worker's organization in the Philippines is "pagbabandon"—awakening, awareness, self-education.

One farmer said that the awakening of the rural workers starts when they become aware of the bigger reality surrounding them. "Now we see more clearly what we suspected all along—that the main causes of our problem include the unjust notion of ownership that we often discuss; the haughty attitudes of the powerful and our own subservient assent to everything they say; the landlord-tenant arrangements that we detest so much; the usurious practices of the middlemen that we abhor: and the mysterious manipulation of price behavior that we find hard to comprehend."[6]

The actions of such people's organizations are manifold:

—cooperative economic projects and training programs;

—technical research oriented toward small farms;

—legal and extra-legal defense action to keep land;

—educational programs to expand and deepen critical awareness among farmers and workers first of all, but also among other sectors of the population.

It is a long and arduous task. For the rural poor it is one from which they are determined never to run back.

No doubt the struggle will be costly. The regime of Ferdinand Marcos declared martial law in 1972, to offer as much incentive as possible to foreign capital. Labor unions came under government control. All strikes, walkouts and picketing were prohibited. Sunday as a compulsory rest day for workers was abolished. Wages were frozen.

For foreign business firms, on the other hand, unrestricted repatriation was guaranteed for earnings and investments. These businesses were exempt from paying taxes in the Philippines on their earnings. Government competition was prohibited. Such a good investment climate both flows from and needs military support. Between 1946 and 1976 the United States provided the Marcos government more than $877 million in military assistance and helped train more than 16,000 Filipino officers and enlisted personnel in U.S. military schools, mostly to control their own citizens.

The mood of many in the Philippines is expressed by one Filipino immigrant to the United States who is sensitive to the relations between the United States and the Philippines.

"President Marcos is the darling of U.S. business. American corporations really gained free reign and power with martial law. They bought up huge parcels of land, opening plantations and growing pineapples there and sending them here. They are perpetuating the colonial mentality and closing their eyes to the suffering of the Filipinos on their land. It is immoral for the United States to establish and protect multinational corporations in a country where the people cannot own their own land. The church should be involved in issues of labor and social justice. Instead it has been captive of the plantation owners, here and in the Philippines. We need to take the lead from our Lord who liberates both the oppressed and the oppressor, who shows us how to take the stranger in and also to free the established powers to act with justice and generosity.'"[7]

CASE STUDY: EL SALVADOR

The scene was grisly. One U.S. Border Patrol officer said it resembled Jonestown—13 swollen bodies, nine of them women, dead, face down, clutching desert shrub for shade in Arizona's sweltering Organ Pipe Cactus National Monument Park near the Mexican border.

The destination was Southern California, where up to one million undocumented aliens are said to reside. Like others before them, they had gathered in a dusty Mexican border town, to be guided across the border by their "coyotes", smugglers of humans for a price.

When the 13 dead and 14 survivors were found in the broiling sun, it was clear that this group was different from others encountered daily by the U.S. Border Patrol. Some carried large sums of cash. They all had paid $1,200—four times the going rate—to be smuggled into the United States. Most surprisingly, only one was from Mexico. The rest were from Central America's tiniest and most densely populated country, El Salvador.[8]

What could have led people to flee so desperately from their own nation?

The roots of the present political crisis in El Salvador go back into the 19th century. Until then, El Salvador's rural Indian population survived on tribal lands farmed in common, which had been granted by the Spanish crown following the conquest. However, independence from Spain in 1821 and the introduction of coffee around 1850 changed all that. Because coffee production was labor intensive, the Indians were forced by the aristocratic Spanish landowners to leave their communal lands and work in the coffee plantations. Uprooted from the land where they had farmed for generations for domestic consumption, the Salvadoran *campesino* (poor farmer) now had to seek wage employment on the newly established coffee farms.

The landowners also needed control over a rural labor force. "Rural judges" were created to determine the labor requirements for the plantations and had the power to force the Indians to work. This system of oligarchic domination of land and labor created the infamous "fourteen families" of El Salvador who emerged by the end of the century in control of both its economic and political life.

On those lands unsuited for coffee, usually barren hills, the campesinos continued to grow basic foods. But because farm plots are so small, the campesinos were forced to seek seasonal employment on coffee and sugar plantations. The oligarchy gained enormously from this seasonal hiring practice. They did not have to maintain the bulk of their harvesting laborers year-round. At the same time, they were always assured a large, unorganized labor supply at times of peak demand.

During this century, the land situation has grown progressively worse. Now 2 percent of El Salvador's 5 million people control 60 percent of all arable land, producing the coffee, cotton and sugar cane that provides the bulk of export earnings.

According to a 1976 study, the number of rural people without access to land either through renting, sharecropping or ownership mushroomed from 12 percent to 40 percent between 1960 and 1975. The result is the lowest per capita food intake in the Western Hemisphere, with three-fourths of the children chronically undernourished and one-half of the work force permanently unemployed or underemployed.

Such conditions have brought about an irresistable demand for basic reforms by the people, a demand that has continued to put pressure on the government. Strict class lines have been drawn in the struggle in El Salvador. The struggle goes back to the early '30s when more than 30,000 campesinos were killed by the Salvadoran government in the suppression of a popular uprising. The military, at the service of the families that control land, industry and commerce, has been in power ever since.

Frightened by the fall of the Somoza regime in Nicaragua, where over half of the land had come under the control of the Somoza family, the United States began to attempt to force the ruling elite in El Salvador to undertake moderate reforms. At the same time, the United States insisted on the suppression of the popular forces that have resorted to guerrilla warfare. The result has been a militarized government controlled by right-wing forces. Though the people went through the form of a national election, the basic structure of control is not changed. The rapidly escalating military aid from the United States seeks to prop up this government which has lost all sense of responsibility toward the vast majority of its people.

In the meantime, the people of El Salvador experience suffering that has few contemporary parallels. Over 10,000 are being killed annually by government military forces, often after extreme torture. Over 200,000 have been uprooted from the countryside mostly through actions of the military. They seek refuge in crowded urban areas with no prospects of employment. Over 300,000 have fled across borders to neighboring countries—Honduras, Costa Rica, Mexico—and exist in squalid refugee camps. Even there they live in fear of harassment, raids and kidnappings by Salvadoran troops. At least another 100,000 have made their way across the U.S. border, seeking safe haven in this country. Instead, they are being apprehended as "illegal aliens" and deported to an uncertain fate, most likely death, in their war-torn country.

The tragedy of the killed and the *desaparecidos* (missing persons) often is muted because their voices can't be heard. Through the throngs of the refugees outsiders can see the dimensions of the Salvadoran drama.

"I swear to you, I wasn't doing anything wrong. I was with a group of young people who were working with a priest in the countryside. He was training us how to teach the campesinos to read and write. One day some soldiers from the National Guard came in and shot him. It was a warning to the rest of us."

—Alicia, a Salvadoran woman in her early twenties.

"About 95 percent of the people I'm working with are Salvadorans. The stories they tell are horrifying, heartbreaking. Fathers, mothers are being executed in front of their kids. I work with them the same way I'd work with Holocaust survivors."

—Joyce, an American social worker at a Hispanic counseling center.

One dimension of the Salvadoran situation that deserves special consideration is the professed "agrarian reform" attempted under the recent junta. News media in the United States have made much of this effort. For example, an editorial in the *New York Times* entitled "Gambling on the Center in El Salvador" states that the Salvadoran government's "ambitious program of land redistribution cuts at the very heart of oligarchic power."[9]

A closer look, however, reveals that the so-called reform actually has been a tool of further repression. Its benefits ultimately have accrued to the Salvadoran oligarchy and its military supporters. Consider:

—The U. S. State Department and the U. S. Embassy in El Salvador imposed the decision to proceed with an agrarian reform upon the Salvadoran Supreme Command, without the knowledge of the Salvadoran Department of Agriculture. They convinced the Salvadorans in control that only through such reform could the armed forces guarantee their victory over the popular revolutionary movement which was spreading and deepening.

—The day after the Agrarian Reform was announced (March 7, 1980), a State of Seige was enacted, justifying itself on the basis of potential threat by certain persons who might try and create "a state of agitation or social unrest." Thus the army would be able to justify any act of institutionalized violence while at the same time rejecting any popular demand or adverse public opinion.

—The land reform set aside most of the nation's coffee land, exempting the major export crop which represents the backbone of the oligarchy's power. Also, landlords soon found ways of subverting the reform. They removed the equipment and machinery from farms, slaughtered cattle prior to the takeover of land, made "sweetheart deals" with the military so that the land stayed in the hands of their larger family and close friends.

—Probably the most vicious aspect of the "agrarian reform" has been its use as a tool of identifying campesino leaders for elimination. This aspect led Jorge Albert Villacorta, assistant minister of agriculture, to resign his position and flee the country. He gave this telling testimony:

"During the first days of reform, five directors and two presidents of new campesino organizations were assassinated and I am informed that this repressive practice continues to increase. Recently, on one of the haciendas of the agrarian reform, uniformed members of the security forces accompanied by someone with a mask over his face, brought the workers together; the masked man was giving orders to the person in charge of the troops and these campesinos were gunned down in front of their coworkers. These bloody acts have been carried out by uniformed members of the National Guard and the hacienda police, accompanied by civilian members of ORDEN (a right-wing paramilitary group), all heavily armed, including support from tanks and heavy equipment."[10]

Thus, whatever success the "agrarian reform" is having in El Salvador is written in blood. The term "reform" has become a mockery of justice, said Archbishop Oscar Romero in a pastoral letter. Within hours he was assassinated while saying mass. The Salvadoran campesinos are ultimately seeking not merely land, but land with justice. They want to participate in the ownership, the management, the direction and the benefits of the land into which they and their forebears have poured so much of their blood, sweat and tears. Because they recognize that this cannot be accomplished as long as the oligarchy or any foreign power dominates their country, they are increasingly joining the revolutionary process.

Undoubtedly much has happened in El Salvador since this writing. Bring the account up to date as well as make a similar study of what is happening in other Central American countries.

CASE STUDY: THE UNITED STATES

To turn from the desperate situations in the Philippines and El Salvador to such a prosperous country as the United States may seem rather disjointed. Yet the phenomenon of landlessness and the factors that have brought it about are much the same.

Over the past several decades, millions of U.S. citizens have been uprooted from the soil. In 1935 approximately 6.8 million farms operated thoughout the U.S. countryside; today fewer than 2.7 million remain. Farms continue to fold at the rate of 1,000 to 1,500 per week. Displaced farmers and their families for the most part migrate to urban areas in search of jobs. Between 1920 and 1960 more than 25 million people left farms for towns and cities.

The process of rural displacement and subsequent urbanization has taken place at such a rapid pace that today 75 percent of U.S. population lives on 2 percent of the land. Urban areas have not coped well with the influx of rural migrants. Unemployment, overcrowding, poor housing, inadequate health care and transportation facilities all testify to the problems created by the uprooting of rural people.

The roots of this displacement run deep. Since World War II, dramatic changes in the U.S. agricultural system have occurred. Agricultural policy has become "get big or get out."

Now, a prevailing view about this agricultural revolution is that it has been beneficial to the U.S. people and the world, providing U.S. citizens with cheap food, helping feed the world, and holding down the U.S. trade deficit. U.S. citizens have come to think of their nation as "the world's breadbasket." However, as Jack Nelson puts it, "the truth is that the breadbasket image is a curious mixture of reality and mirage. The U.S. food system is like a nicely painted house with a faulty foundation. It looks good from a distance, but may be incapable of weathering the storm."[11]

The decline of the family farm has become a matter of national concern. Traditionally, the family farm has been viewed as being as American as motherhood and apple pie. Thomas Jefferson saw how vital the connection was between the family farm and the preservation of the American political system: "The widely dispersed ownership of land by the tiller is the American ideal and a safeguard for democracy."

Why break those family farmers regarded as the backbone of the nation? Ostensibly in the name of greater efficiency of food production. With the shift to agriculture as a capital intensive, high technology, mass production business, it is now possible for one U.S. farmer, with tremendous investment of machinery, cash and chemicals, to produce food for 57 people.

The social costs, however, have been devastating. As Wendell Berry, a farmer and poet, writes: "It has been made possible by the substitution of energy for knowledge, of methodology for care, of technology for morality. This 'accomplishment' is not primarily the work of farmers—who have been, by and large, its victims—but a large collaboration of corporations, university specialists, and government agencies. It is therefore an agricultural development not motivated by agricultural aims or disciplines, but by the ambitions of merchants, industrialists, bureaucrats and academic careerists. We should not be surprised to find that its effect on both the farm land and the farm people has been ruinous."[12]

As might be expected, the impact has been most severe upon non-white rural people. At the mercy of economic and political systems over which they have had little or no control, rural blacks in the southern United States have lost their land at over twice the rate of white farmers.

According to a 1970 U.S. Agricultural Census, between 1950 and 1970 the amount of black-owned farm land declined from 12 million to 5.5 million acres, a loss of more than 50 percent. In 1920, 925,000 blacks operated farms in this country, 90 percent of which were in the South. As of 1978, only 57,000 black-operated farms remained. One of the hardest won victories in the battle against slavery—black-owned land—is now being reversed. A whole way of life for black farmers is being lost.

Native Americans likewise have suffered from this agricultural revolution. These people who once roamed free across this continent now, if they are to maintain their distinctive identity, are restricted to less than 3 percent of the country's less productive soil.

Now, though 400,000 acres of Indian land are classified as agricultural, 73 percent of this income goes to non-Indian operators. Farmers, usually with large holdings, lease the land from its Indian owners for only a fraction of what the lease is actually worth. The main reason is that such large landowners are able to secure governmental help in the form of loans, irrigation rights and technical assistance. Increasingly, Native Americans must struggle against the encroachment of large energy corporations seeking coal and uranium.

The impact has not been limited to the non-white U.S. population. Appalachia itself is a case study of economic colonialism not too different from that which prevails in many nations of the Third World. The area has great wealth in mineral resources producing $1.5 billion worth of coal in a year. An extensive network of railroads and highly sophisticated machinery and industries links it to the largest corporations in the world. Yet, one finds great poverty, substandard housing, hunger, poor health, low levels of education, low rate of skilled labor and constant migration out of the area. How can these incongruities be explained? Are the people living in this area some type of cultural throwback? Or are they the victims of an "internal colonialism" that has systematically controlled and exploited the majority of the people?[13]

A study on land ownership patterns and their impacts on Appalachian communities, completed in 1981, provides clues. Based on a detailed study of 80 counties in Appalachia, the report documents in specific detail what had long been known in a general way:

—The ownership of land and minerals in Appalachia is highly concentrated in the hands of a few owners.

—Three-fourths of Appalachia's land and mineral resources are absentee-owned.

—Large corporations dominate the ownership picture in much of Appalachia.

—Little land is owned by or accessible to local people.

—The absentee corporations and individuals in whose hands land and mineral ownership is concentrated pay such meager taxes on their holdings that local governments and Appalachian people are chronically impoverished.

The study confirms that Appalachia is suffering the same kind of agricultural upheaval as is being experienced by Third World Nations.

CASE STUDY: CANADA

Canada's land mass is huge, almost 2.3 billion acres. Only 24 million acres is in areas with favorable climate. This means less than 2 percent of the total land area is suitable for agricultural production.

Familiar issues face Canadians in relation to the ownership and use of their land—concentrated ownership, corporate farming, high land prices, cities gobbling up land, disappearing family farms, unfair treatment of ethnic minority landholders and laborers.

The results of Canada's land crisis are also felt by the rural family. Small communities are struggling for survival and some are dying. Farmers are being forced off the land; the larger farming operations are taking over. Farm laborers are being replaced by machines. Persons once firmly attached to the land are being uprooted—fleeing to the urban centers in search of a job, a chance to survive.

The family farm is disappearing in Canada and with its death farm families are being uprooted.

In 1941 there were 138,700 farms, with an average size of 432 acres, in the province of Saskatchewan. Thirty years later the average farm size had almost doubled to 845 acres and the number of farms had decreased to 77,000. During that period the farm population fell from 514,700 to 233,800. The price of land quadrupled in about the same period of time.

Saskatchewan faces another land use problem. Over one-third of the farmers there are near retirement age. Prices make it difficult for young men and women to begin farming.

A Land Bank Act was passed to help preserve family farms by allowing the government to buy land from leaving or retiring farmers and lease it back, on a long-term basis, to those wishing to begin farming. But thus far only 1 percent of Saskatchewan's farmland has been purchased because of low land bank budgets and high levels of competition for land. Prices continue to increase and the number of farmers shrink.

Saskatchewan isn't the only province where small farms are becoming history. Jim Tuininga, former executive director of the Christian Farmers' Federation of Alberta (CFF), sees both speculation and higher land prices as taking their toll on small farm operations.

"I have a friend who bought three quarter sections outside Edmonton and had to pay $1,000 an acre. It's very hard to recoup that kind of expense through agriculture. Some solution must be found: one that does not take initiative from the small private farmer. It is inevitable that government must take a larger role in regulating land use. Without some kind of control over speculation and farm size, small farmers will continue to be forced from the land."[14]

With the loss of small farming operations comes the loss of small rural businesses, rural schools, a whole way of life.

> Think about land ownership patterns in local counties or in your state. How have they changed over the past three decades? What groups have been uprooted? What are the critical issues now being faced?

WHAT CAN THE CHURCHES DO?

A Christian leader from India is quoted as saying, "You American Christians are great in a crisis but poor in a struggle." North Americans confront the monumental problems related to the world's landless people with a realization that Christian response requires much more than simply a momentary expression of compassion. Rather, Christians are called to join a struggle, the struggle of uprooted persons to claim their homes and land.

The church in some parts of the world has learned this lesson at great cost. In numerous countries the church has awakened anew to the call of the Gospel to stand with the poor. This is not consistently the case. Often the institutional church is divided and ambivalent. Yet a committed community has emerged that chooses to seek economic and social justice for the poor.

Certainly this is true in Latin America. Long before the historic Catholic declarations of Medellin (1968) and Pueblo (1979), many Christians in Latin America had to assume responsibility for Christian social action on behalf of poor people. An irreversible dynamic was released in the region. The church became the catalyst of those winds of change that are now sweeping that region and disrupting longstanding patterns of injustice and exploitation.

The church has changed in Central America. Beginning in the Roman Catholic "base communities" among the poor and spreading into Protestant circles, the church has come to see the present condition as a scandal, as a contradiction to Christian faith, as sin.

The church has paid a price. Leaders of the Salvadoran Catholic Church stated: "The church cannot avoid persecution when it is faithful to this option: Christ was accused before Pilate because 'He stirs up the people, teaching throughout all Judea.' He who healed and preached to the poor, went around doing good, had compassion on the multitudes and did miracles to benefit the poor, was crucified because he caused disturbances by pointing out sin, injustice and violence in the nation."[15]

Beginning with the National Council of Churches of Christ in the U.S.A. and reflected in actions of several denominations, resolutions have been addressed to the U.S. government to end all military aid to the Salvadoran government and to promote a political settlement in that country "with full respect and participation of all concerned." Likewise, in Canada the Inter-Church Committee on Human Rights in Latin America and Canadian church leaders from a number of denominations have made repeated presentations to the Canadian government, opposing military "solutions" in El Salvador and urging Canada to denounce human rights violations and embody a concern for human rights in its foreign policy. Individual Christians are critically needed to respond to their elected officials when action is called for.

Partnership with other Christians in such areas is also shown through support of efforts to relieve the massive human suffering, especially among the uprooted persons of the world. Programs for Salvadoran refugees in Honduras, Costa Rica and Mexico are being implemented by Christian agencies in those countries. These agencies include Catholics and Protestants banded together to protect, feed and shelter the refugees.

Church groups in the Southwest have mobilized to help these Salvadorans and to try to halt their deportation. In Arizona, the Tucson Ecumenical Council has spearheaded a drive to raise collatoral from local churches and individuals to bail Salvadorans out of Border Patrol detention camps and provide them with legal help to prevent their deportation. Some church members have even offered their homes and properties as guarantees. Some Salvadoran asylum-seekers are known to be suffering lack of food, shelter and other basic necessities in silence because of their fear of detection, apprehension and deportation.

Churches in Canada have an opportunity not available to those in the United States since the Canadian government has decided to admit refugees from El Salvador and Guatemala. The guidelines issued to the churches by Canadian immigration are revealing:

"We would like your efforts in aid of refugee resettlement to be concentrated as much as possible on people who are in need of protection and who would be in a particular danger should, at some future time, they be required to return to El Salvador."[16]

Yet all these efforts, as noble and needed as they are, still do not address the root, the crying need of the world's landless people for genuine agrarian reform. The Brandt Report, entitled *North/South: A Programme For Survival*, summarizes what this entails:

"Agrarian reform is a critical means to benefit the poor—though naturally the measures needed differ from country to country. In some areas the key issue is reform of tenancy to give greater security of tenure. In others it is to divide large parcels of land among those who can farm it more intensively. Yet others require consolidation measures to overcome the effect of excessive fragmentation of holdings which has already occurred. All these can increase the incentive for farmers' investment."[17]

How can the churches help in this move toward agrarian reform? Undoubtedly one of the most effective ways is to work with rural people's movements through which the poor people of the world are struggling to achieve justice in their land. Throughout the world, rural people's movements are emerging even under the most oppressive regimes. In the Americas, Indians and campesinos are banding together to save their small plots. In Africa, certain freedom movements have been deeply rooted in rural transformation. Rural people's movements in Asia are a major force for land reform.

In the United States, farm workers have organized themselves into bargaining units to confront the established system of crew leaders and large growers. Black farmers are forming cooperatives to keep their land and to develop appropriate agricultural techniques and effective marketing systems. Native Americans are working together to resist the pressures of large corporations so that their land will be used for agriculture and development of their own people.

The church, a "transnational corporation" with a focus on people rather than profits, has an opportunity everywhere to work toward a more active solidarity with people's movements and organizations.

Agricultural Missions is one agency which brings together representatives of both Protestant denominations and Catholic orders in the United States and Canada. Founded in 1934, Agricultural Missions originally helped denominational boards send out rural missionaries. In time its focus shifted to training local pastors in rural churches and helping develop a theology of rural life and worship. It also provided programs of technical assistance to Christian agriculturalists in developing countries.

But in the early 1970s, it became evident that all this was not enough. The plight of the world's rural poor was becoming increasingly desperate. Benton Rhoades, executive secretary of Agricultural Missions, says, "It was useless to speak of minitractors, hybrid seeds or breeding techniques with the rural poor, if those small farmers were unsure of their land ownership, or trapped between tenancy and loan sharks. It was ridiculous to push new varieties when a farmer's biggest problem was not seedlings, but a place to plant them. It was difficult to bring people together when military rule had soldiers in every village and land-grabbers fast behind them. We discovered another important lesson—that we, North Americans, with all of our technical training—had more to learn from village people than we could possibly teach."[18]

On the basis of that realization, Agricultural Missions completely changed its goals, its strategies, its working style. It took on the task of both being and building the bridge between the church and rural people's movements. Rather than sending "experts" overseas, it sought out local people's organizations, assisted their leaders, supported cooperative economic projects and training programs, provided help for legal defense action for land ownership and human rights, and undertook the monumental task of building regional and global networks linking together these groups who were struggling toward the common goal of land and justice.

After almost a decade in this new approach, a consultation was called in April 1979. The meeting brought together a rare combination of people, church leaders from North America, representatives of overseas churches and leaders of rural people's movements from around the globe. Its "Message to the Churches," outlined several directives, including the following:

—The churches must support decolonialization efforts throughout the world, including the colonized areas and people within the territorial boundaries of the United States and Canada.

—The churches must mount a serious education program designed to lead to a more active solidarity with people's movements and organizations. They should draw on the people's movements for analysis and critique. They should recognize the need for a continuing reflection/action process on all levels.

—The churches must critically examine and radically change their domestic church life to express their solidarity with poor and oppressed persons. Particular attention should be paid to changes in relation to budgets for maintenance, land and property holdings, investments in multinational corporations, elitist membership in church boards, vested interests in projects, clergy classism, a theology of neutrality.

—The churches must support the struggle of Native Americans for justice. They should enable interchange between Indian communities throughout the American continents, supporting, preserving and strengthening their culture and promoting their full possession and development of their own land.

—The churches must avoid supporting projects that are based solely on charity or which tend to reinforce the status quo, directing their resources to those working for permanent change in favor of human life.

—The churches must set a special and urgent priority to halt poor persons' loss of land.[19]

Little can be added to that message, except to apply it to the life of the church in every local community, congregation and church agency. If one looks across the nation, numerous groups are raising the critical questions about the economic and military policies of the world's rich nations. The policies are uprooting people and creating poverty and hunger. The voices of these uprooted persons must be heard. Numerous organizations are striving to conserve and protect precious land and water resources for the benefit of all the people. They need strength. Numerous agencies are helping poor persons to become self-sufficient. They must have support.

Within easy range of almost every church, there are self-help organizations of the poor—agricultural cooperatives, food co-ops, community gardens and canneries, farmworker organizations, farmers' marketing projects and many others. You can work on positive alternatives to uprootedness. You can become an advocate and supporter.

Then Christians may say with the prophet Amos, "Let justice roll down like waters, and righteousness like an ever-flowing stream." (Amos 5:24)

UNHCR/12177/M. Vanappelghem

Guatemalan refugee attends religious ceremony in Mexico.

Photo by Bob East, Miami Herald

Haitian refugee child now living in United States.

Chapter Five:
Searching For Work,
Searching For Roots

Jesus radically redefined "neighbor" in the story of the Good Samaritan. (Luke 10:25-37) In response to the question, "Who is my neighbor?" Jesus tells a story about one who "proved neighbor." Instead of providing a legal limit for neighborliness, Jesus took off all the limits with a picture of neighbor-love as open-ended as the world's need.

It was no accident that Jesus chose to define "neighbor" in terms of a Samaritan, representing those people so near and yet so far from the Jews. There was a clear-cut border between "us" and "them." "They" were despised and contact with "them" was regarded as a serious source of corruption. But, in Jesus' story, a Jew is dependent upon a Samaritan! Indeed, it is a Samaritan who comes to the rescue after two very religious Jews pass by the suffering victim "on the other side."

Question: Who is my neighbor?

Answer: The one who needs my compassion and the one whose compassion I need.

Lesson: Go and do. Wherever need and compassion meet, the relationship of neighbor is established.

How would this story sound if it were taking place in this time and place? What if it became the story of the "Good Mexican" or the "Good Haitian"? What would be involved in a really "good neighbor" policy toward the people on U.S. and Canadian borders? The problem of joblessness in the Third World spills into the First World as people search for work and a chance at survival.

"THE BAREST HOPE OF A JOB"

The city of Juarez sits with its open wounds like a beggar at the temple gate of El Paso. The Third World is face to face with the first world over a demilitarized zone of putrid water patrolled on both sides by border guards.

About 25,000 persons perch on the barren arid hills at the fraying hem of Juarez. They haul the polluted water up from the Rio Grande River and huddle under whatever wood, tin and paper they can scrounge to make shelters. They are not here for the lovely view of booming El Paso.

"Coming from a Mexican heartland that is suffocating under the burden of 50 percent of its people either underemployed (working for wages too low to provide basic food and shelter needs) or unemployed, they come for the barest hope of a job from their affluent Texan neighbors. Discarded cardboard boxes now disappear from the driveways of new ranch homes in El Paso and reappear as shelters for the desperate people on the other side of the border. . . . Meanwhile the homeless, jobless squatters along this tarnished border, and the millions more without jobs or hope south of the border, have only one means of entry. It is through the water."[1]

—Thomas Bentz, *The New Immigrants: Portraits in Passage*

The migration of workers across national boundaries has assumed unprecedented proportions in the last decade. The increase is a symptom of a world economy that is fundamentally askew, an economy in which gross income disparities both within and among countries have become widening chasms. In the developing countries of the southern hemisphere, over one third of the working age population, some 300 million people, are already underemployed or unemployed. In the industrial countries of the northern hemisphere, while there is periodic unemployment in the 8 to 10 percent range, there is often a demand for cheap seasonal labor which requires little of the employer. Like positive and negative charges of a battery, these forces create a powerful magnetic field in which migration occurs.

This phenomenon is not only national, but global. At the present there are an estimated 20 million migrant workers in the world. An estimated six million are in the United States, about half of them coming from Mexico. The number of migrant workers in Western Europe has varied from two million in the '60s, to six million in the early '70s, to about five million at the present. Since the early '70s large numbers of migrant workers have gone to the oil exporting countries of the Middle East, about three million are there now. South Africa has for many years attracted labor for mining operations, around 400,000 migrant workers are there at the present. These laborers are from its neighboring black nations.

In all these situations, the rich countries have the upper hand, controlling the number and character of migrant employment and the duration of the migrant workers' stay. Much of the demand has been "structural," that is, coming from industries that cannot attract citizens of the rich countries or that will not make the commitments necessary to keep them.

Migrant labor in many countries is treated as a temporary work force, a spigot to be turned on and off according to the needs of the employer. No wonder that much migration takes place under illegal and abusive conditions. Traffickers organize this trade for their own gain. Migrant workers are often work under sub-human working conditions, in wretched housing, with meager wages, without health insurance or social security, and with no recourse for appeal.

Meanwhile, the countries which the migrants have left receive a mixed blessing. They may gain from the jobs provided to some of their underemployed. Potentially the training and skills acquired by workers may benefit their nation when later they return. The nation may also benefit from the money sent back by migrants. These funds have become major foreign exchange earnings for many developing countries. However, such countries must be prepared to be buffeted by the fluctuation in the demand for migrant labor.

In a time of general economic recession they may find their ranks of unemployed swollen by the influx of workers who have returned home. Often those nations have lost, at least for a while, the young, the ambitious, the skilled and semi-skilled persons who are so badly needed by their homelands.

The various countries receiving the migrants differ widely in their treatment of migrant laborers. Some admit them to citizenship in due course and, in the meantime, allow them some of the rights that go with it. Within the European community, migrant workers from other member countries enjoy the same rights as domestic workers. The International Labor Organization has formulated norms which provide for the respect of the basic rights of all migrant workers and ensure that migrants and their families get fair treatment in living and working conditions, in social security, health and safety. Under these guidelines they are allowed to reunite their families, to preserve their ethnic identity, and to join trade unions. Unfortunately, these norms have been ratified by only a small number of countries. The United States and Canada have not ratified these norms.

South Africa illustrates starkly the worst side of the immigration policy of a receiving country. The black workers have neither permanent rights of residence in the place where they work, nor a voice in its political affairs. "Foreign labor" has worked so well for South Africa that the government has now embarked on a systematic program to turn a sizable number of indigenous black citizens into foreigners via the notorious "homeland policy," whereby the government has created artificial mini-states for various tribal groups.

Black people still work in white South African homes, factories, mines and farms. Yet the "foreign" status of these black workers means they will not be allowed to live permanently near their work place nor have other rights afforded to citizens. This means that families are often separated as some members must travel and remain for weeks or months at their work while others remain at "home" in the created mini-states. Some shanty towns built by families around the work sites have been bulldozed away and the families sent "home" or arrested.

Illegal immigration of laborers into the United States is prosecuted with so little effect as to almost seem an endorsement. Some people believe that this fulfills a function very similar to that of the South Africa Homeland Policy. That is, it provides U.S. employers with a cheap, passive labor force with no political rights. This belief is supported by the fact that waves of enforcement seem to follow the ups and downs of U.S. economy rather closely. The immigration laws rise in public esteem along with the unemployment rate. Expelling foreign workers is a rarity in other receiving countries, even in the most difficult times. The United States comes perhaps closest to such a stance, since a large part of its migrant labor population is forced into the shadow of illegality.

The Brandt Report concludes its section on "International Migration of Labor" with this statement:

'The migration of people in search of better opportunities to make a living is an essential aspect of development and change and has been so throughout history. We are still far from a shared understanding of the principles that should guide international migration. In the meantime, the objective must be to build, on the basis of the interests of the countries concerned, a framework that is more just and equitable than the present one.'[2]

MEXICAN MIGRATION TO THE UNITED STATES

When people in the United States consider the matter of migration of labor across national borders, one picture immediately comes to mind: Mexicans wading across the Rio Grande, along the 2,000-mile border between Mexico and the United States.

The picture is an overly simplistic one. Each year 82 million people cross the border legally, a quarter of a million each day. The southern border of the United States with Mexico is the world's busiest border; no two countries anywhere else approach this volume of traffic.

The real "border" between the two countries is of an economic nature: the vast income difference that exists north and south of the Rio Grande. In 1979, the average per capita income in Mexico was $1,538 while that in the United States was $10,536. The difference is compounded by the unequal distribution within Mexico, with the gap progressively widening.

The push factors which force people out of Mexico include the endemic poverty of large numbers of persons; the high rates of unemployment, 26 percent in 1976, and underemployment, 50 percent in the same year; and misdirected government aid and economic policies.

The pull factors that make the United States an attractive destination are greater availability of jobs, higher wage levels and U.S. dependence on recruitment of cheap non-union labor.

How many are involved in this migration? The truth is that no one knows. It is evident, even from Immigration and Naturalization Service estimates, that Mexicans probably make up no more than half of the annual flow of "undocumented" persons into the United States.

The great debate, however, concerns the number of Mexican citizens who reside illegally in the United States. Recent estimates have been as high as 12 million. The U.S. Immigration and Naturalization Service (INS) released such as estimate in the mid-1970s. On the basis of those figures great public attention was created, prompting talk of a "silent invasion" by illegal aliens. Unfortunately, Congress began to create new legislation on this basis even though it was shown that the figures were grossly inaccurate.

In 1980, the U.S. Census Bureau reduced the upper estimate to six million. A Census Bureau expert has estimated that the number may be no higher than three million and as low as 1.5 million, a figure which comes fairly close to the Mexican government estimate.

Some facts about this migration are certain. The average length of stay is probably less than six months, though persons may make annual or frequent trips over an extended time. The return flow to Mexico is estimated to be as high as 88 percent so that for many the border is a "revolving door." A composite profile of the average migrant would indicate a male, from a rural area, unmarried, with only three or four years of formal schooling and little or no command of English. The migrant workers who come to the United States are the most youthful, vigorous and resourceful of Mexico's rural people. Needless to say, the absence of such persons from their Mexican communities removes a vital resource from community life and development. However, the most common motivation for coming to the United States is to earn money to help their families acquire land in their rural Mexican region. Thus the families can escape the poverty which plagues those areas.

Which leads back to the "misdirected government policies" mentioned earlier. To meet its need for capital for rapid industrialization, Mexico has sought to gain foreign exchange by increasing agricultural exports. When the "Bracero" program which allowed Mexicans to work in the United States came to an end in 1965, U.S. agribusiness firms decided to go to Mexico where there would be an unlimited supply of cheap labor. Though prohibited from owning farms, these firms were allowed to make contract arrangements in some of Mexico's most fertile irrigated agricultural areas. Mexico now supplies between 50 and 60 percent of all fresh vegetables eaten in the United States between December and May.

A major transformation in Mexican agriculture occurred. The best lands became wealthy centers of capital-intensive modern U.S. agribusiness. Rural poor persons were pushed off their land more and more often. Some have become farm laborers. But of each dollar spent on Mexican tomatoes in the United States, only 11 cents go to the men, women and children who plant, weed, pick and pack the crop. Thus, U.S. consumers compete directly with the rural poor of Mexico for the fruit of their land and labor. This is, of course, a highly unequal battle.

The point of the story is this: The undocumented workers coming into the United States have been displaced by an agricultural system created by the U.S. and Mexican governments for the benefit of U.S. agribusiness and U.S. consumers. They cross the border in search of work and some way out of the poverty that grips their lives.

What are the policy options for the United States in dealing with Mexican migration? The following represent a group of the major possibilities:

Close the border to illegal entry. Attorney General William French Smith says, "America has lost control of its own borders. Enforcement efforts must prove equal to the goals of our new policy, to regain control of our own borders." This is an option which sounds simple and can gain a degree of popular support, especially in a time of increasing unemployment. However, the financial and social costs would be enormous. Expenditures for the Border Patrol would have to be vastly increased, causing virtual militarization of 2,000 miles of U.S. territory. The government would intrude into the lives and civil rights of many citizens and legal residents. The Mexican government would be displeased, threatening future U.S. access to needed petroleum and gas supplies.

Besides, it would not succeed in stemming the tide of illegal immigration from other countries, which would increase to provide the cheap labor sought by certain industries. U.S. citizens would pick up the tab and gain nothing.

Open the border and enforce labor legislation. Acquiring legal status, immigrant workers would not be forced to seek the help of coyotes (smugglers) to get them across the border. They would not need to endure exploitation by employers out of fear of being deported. Immigrant workers might also be more disposed to join unions. Such potential benefits would be realized only if a relaxed border policy were coupled with strict state and federal enforcement of wage, hour and work environment laws. This would not solve the dilemma regarding those who come seeking domestic unskilled jobs where wage and hour laws do not apply.

Institute a guest worker program. In a sense, the Bracero program, 1942-1964, was a guest worker program. Today, the United States has a similar, though more limited temporary worker program for agriculture. Commonly known as the H-2 program, 30,000 foreign workers are admitted annually, mostly from Caribbean nations, on documentation that U.S. workers are unavailable. The H-2 worker is under contract for a specific job, at stated terms and for a specified period. However, organized labor has attacked the H-2 program on grounds that it has been manipulated by employers to deny jobs to U.S. workers.

Establish temporary worker quotas, along with stricter sanctions against employers who evade labor laws. This approach would grant a Temporary Worker Visa to a specified number of Mexican applicants, annually determined in relation to historic experience and U.S. labor needs. Holders of the visa would be legally entitled to enter the United States in search of work, as many now do illegally, and to remain as long as evidence of employment could be given. At the same time, legal penalties severe enough to have a deterrent effect would be imposed upon those who employ undocumented workers.

Such a system would permit a legal flow of labor to enter the United States with a minimum of bureaucratic structures. Workers could move freely in search of employment. As always, there would be disadvantages. Employer groups would resist legislation imposing such penalties. Some labor unions would oppose legal sanction for a competitive labor force. Most controversial is the necessity of some form of identification establishing eligibility for work for both citizens and noncitizens. Such a "national identity card" raises the fear of increasing government control.

Participate in the economic development of Mexico. The previous options focus on controlling the pull factors which make the United States attractive to Mexican workers. Any of these may be combined with the option of reducing the push factors that drive people from Mexico in search of work. Only when Mexico has a more dynamic and diversified economy capable of using more of its employable people will the migration lessen.

Mexico has confidence its economic woes can be solved by its own resources, especially with its fast growing petroleum exports. The role for U.S. cooperation in Mexico's economic development can be supportive. The United States can cooperate in ways other than simply transferring capital. By reducing tariffs and other trade barriers to Mexican-made goods, export production can be increased, creating jobs. Restructuring the agricultural sector is a major key to Mexico's future development. The implementation of a land reform program would provide viable farm units for a larger portion of the rural population. This entails the most important contribution the United States can make, namely, helping to increase the social accountability of U.S.-based corporations.

Which option or combination of options should the church favor and support?

THE "BLACK BOAT PEOPLE" FROM HAITI

"Late at night, as the lights go out in the expensive beach homes on the south shores of Florida, small rickety sailboats slowly approach the deserted beaches. Within a stone's throw of the walled-in mansions, women and children slip over the sides of sailboats and drop into the water. Just a few hundred feet from the beach, some children, having just survived 900 miles at sea, will flail and drown. Unable to swim, they lose their quest for freedom in the last 100 feet.

"These are the so-called 'black boat people,' refugees from the Haitian government of President-for-life Jean-Claude Duvalier. Most of the drownings go unreported; some estimates number them in the thousands. While President Jimmy Carter called for 'safety and order' in the exodus of Cuban refugees, who travel 90 miles in power boats chartered in Miami, little concern was expressed for the black boat people, who cross hundreds of miles of wind swept seas in dismally small and overcrowded wooden sailboats."[3]

—Peter A. Sohey, *Refugee and Human Rights Newsletter,* Winter 1981.

Haitians have been fleeing a land of desperate poverty and oppression for over a decade now. Only recently have they gained national visibility. Some 40,000-50,000 Haitians arrived illegally in the United States between 1972 and 1982, according to U.S. Immigration and Naturalization Service estimates. About 20,000 of them are hidden in the "Little Haiti" section of Miami. More than 3,200 of them are in detention camps as of this writing. More than 1,000 a month continue to come.

Yet, only one in 20 Haitians who seek refuge outside of their homeland come to the United States. Over one million Haitians of a nation of five million are dispersed throughout the Caribbean basin. Many of them are in small nations which can ill afford such an influx. The Caribbean Basin as a whole is a whirlpool of migration. The Caribbean people move among the West Indies and Central America, seeking employment and a better livelihood as their own nations experience staggering socioeconomic problems. In times such as this, the United States appears on the horizon as "the golden land," the mecca for those who dare to seek it.

The situation from which Haitians are fleeing is far more complex. The poverty of Haiti is the worst in the western hemisphere, with an average per capita income of $260 per year. Eighty percent of its people are among the "poorest of the poor," and at least that many are illiterate. Eighty-three percent of the children under five years old are suffering from malnutrition. The streets of its cities are filled with beggars. People bathe in stench-ridden open sewers.

Why? Why does Haiti suffer so much? Haiti suffers under a dictatorship which exists through the permission and support of the United States. U.S. domination over Haiti was first established in 1915 when U.S. Marines began a 19-year occupation of the country. For the past 23 years, the United States has supported the Duvalier family's bloody and sometimes precarious rule. Money, weapons and training have flowed from Washington, D.C., to the Haitian National Palace.

Support for the Duvalier regime has two purposes. First, U.S. foreign policy strategists are concerned lest the Caribbean, traditionally an American stronghold, become a "Marxist Sea." Seventy-five percent of U.S. oil imports and 90 percent of its imported strategic minerals must travel the sea lanes past the Caribbean islands. Haiti happens to be right in the middle of the Caribbean.

Second, there is a concern about the protection of U.S. investments in the Caribbean and Central America which total approximately $13.7 billion. The Haitian government offers U.S. investors incredibly low labor costs—$2.20 per day. "There are almost 300 U.S. factories in Haiti," says Haitian Father Antoine Adrien, "and the profit is unbelievable."

The AFL-CIO has taken the position that American multinational corporations have exported jobs and production facilities to Haiti in a "disgraceful example . . . of mismanaged U.S. laws and policies."

Unfortunately, only a small percent of the profit of such industries stays in Haiti. What does stay flows directly into the hands of a small group of Haitian wealthy families—.8 percent of the population controls 43.7 percent of all income in the country. Since 1969, with the buildup of U.S. big business involvement in Haiti, the personal dictatorship of "Papa Doc" Francois Duvalier has changed to a class dictatorship built around the ruthless regime of his son "Baby Doc" Jean-Claude Duvalier.

The flight of Haitians from this oppression has brought U.S. human rights policy into direct conflict with U.S. foreign and immigration policies. As the United States manifests a declining commitment to the area of international human rights, military governments will get the message that their own concern about human rights can slow down. Then refugee flows from countries like Haiti will undoubtedly increase.

The U.S. government does not want to alienate President-for-Life Duvalier. Thus, it is forced to reject the claims of Haitians to be considered politically oppressed people and to characterize them as "economically motivated migrants." Said one INS official: "It's a simple issue as to whether they are being persecuted in Haiti . . . Clearly they're not. They are just poor people coming here to work—just like the Mexicans."

This claim is made despite the fact that in November 1980 some 500 suspected opponents of the regime were rounded up and thrown in jail, some of them not to be heard from again. They included journalists, human rights advocates, students, trade unionists, and those engaged in development activities in the countryside.

A police state is maintained. The notorious Ton-Ton Macoutes, the official name is "Volunteers for National Security," carry out a reign of terror and extortion throughout the countryside, without legal constraints, answering only to the Duvaliers. Yet, the INS still claims there is no persecution.

The U.S. federal court has recognized that Haiti's economic problems "are the manifestations of oppression" and the economic stagnation in Haiti "is demonstrably an outgrowth of Duvalier politics." In such a situation, the distinction between "political" and "economic" refugees becomes meaningless.

Haitians in search of jobs and a chance to determine their own future have not found a place in the United States. But the joblessness of these persons destines them to search for work and for some guarantee of survival. There is no hope for them in their homeland, so they must leave their homeland. They have discovered that emotional, cultural, family and community roots cannot replace basic food and shelter. When the decision must be made they become part of the world's up-rooted people.

Almost every denomination has some mission involvement in Haiti. In addition to the predominant Catholic church, some 250 denominations are working in the area of Port-au-Prince alone, according to Father Antoine Adrien. What relationship is there between this missionary effort and the political situation in Haiti? What is the mission of the church in relation to the refugees from Haiti coming to this country?

BUT WHAT ABOUT U.S. AND CANADIAN CITIZENS WHO ARE JOBLESS?

When 29-year-old Dock Green lost his job on the management training squad at a fried chicken franchise in Dallas, the first telephone call he made was to the U.S. Immigration and Naturalization Service. "I realized I was in trouble right from the start when I saw that I was the only one there who spoke English. Everyone else spoke only Spanish," Green said. "I kept complaining to my boss that all these people were illegal aliens, and he didn't want to do anything about it.

"I have nothing against those people, but every day we had people coming in asking about jobs, and it's a pitiful shame to have people who are born and raised here be out of work, and have these illegal aliens taking their job. To me, the law means what it says, and if those people are illegal, then the law should be obeyed."[4]

Green is not alone in his frustration. Immigrants in general, and illegal aliens in particular, are subjected to rising criticism as they play an increasingly visible role in the job market. The degree of criticism increases relative to the unemployment rate, which at this point has reached 9 percent in the United States.

Of course, attitudes vary tremendously according to the impact on different groups within a society. Most U.S. Hispanic leaders insist the impact of these workers is essentially benign. They say that Mexican workers, for example, do the jobs most U.S. citizens don't want—the low paying, low skill, dead-end jobs. Yet they are essential for the functioning of the U.S. economy in such areas as the harvesting of crops, the garment industry and restaurant business. Even if all undocumented workers were expelled, they claim, the basic economic conditions creating low paying employment and unemployment would remain. In fact, unemployment might increase, for many regular jobs might fold if the base provided by such low-income jobs should disappear.

Further, they argue, refugees and undocumented aliens, far from being a drain on the economy, actually contribute significantly to it. A 1978 U.S. Department of Labor study reported that, although almost 80 percent of undocumented workers paid federal income and Social Security taxes, less than 5 percent received any type of social services. As for refugees, a study conducted for the Select Commission on Immigration and Refugee Policy indicated that it usually takes less than six years for an immigrant family to earn as much as a native family, paying into the treasury more in taxes than they take out in service.

Immigrants take their share of blame for unemployment in Canada, too. A United Church of Canada paper on immigration and employment says:

" 'When all else fails, blame it on the immigrant' has been a recurrent theme over the past 100 years of Canadian immigration policy.

"Immigrants, especially blacks and Asians, because they are highly visible and since they often take jobs that Canadians refuse to do, easily become the focus of frustrations and antagonisms for Canadians who feel fearful and threatened and know no other outlet for their emotions."

A Canadian television survey several years ago in Toronto, Montreal and Vancouver indicated that a majority of Canadians samples are at least a little disturbed by present immigration trends. Asked if increasing immigration levels were considered a threat to Canadian jobs, 65 percent said yes.[5]

For most middle and upper class U.S. and Canadian citizens, refugees and undocumented migrants have had relatively little direct impact. They have experienced almost no job competition. The cheap labor supply has probably benefited them as consumers. In the Southwest especially, the willingness of undocumented workers to work at sub-minimum wages makes it possible for many middle class families to have household help. Some businesses claim they have been able to maintain a level of profitability, and in some cases to avoid closure, only because of labor cost savings achieved by using such workers. Other experts refute this claim, saying businesses would have less profit but few would close.

The one exception to the above attitude among middle class U.S. and Canadian citizens is the increasing racism which has become evident in particular areas.

The same television study quoted earlier also showed marked racial considerations. "While the sample is small, the results are none the less distressing in their racist implications," the United Church paper says. "Asked to name preferred source countries for immigration to Canada, 46 percent of the respondents said they did not want any Africans, 42 percent said they did not want any Asians, 36 percent said they did not want any Caribbeans and 34 percent said they did not want any Latin Americans."

The Ku Klux Klan is among those groups calling for a halt to all nonwhite immigration. In 1979, members of the KKK held an open demonstration at the California-Mexico border to protest what they called "the brown tide." Reports persist of Klansmen in Southern California acting as vigilante groups to apprehend and expel illegal Mexican migrants.

Some other groups join in responding negatively to the influx of foreign workers. Organized labor is a shrinking portion of the labor force, with fewer than 20 percent of all workers in unions. Some unions are convinced that illegal aliens have lowered the wage scale, reduced the possibilities of organizing in certain areas and generally increased unemployment for citizens.

The United Farm Worker Union, however, has consistently supported total amnesty for undocumented workers living in the United States. The union objects to the use of undocumented workers as strike breakers. The undocumented workers lack status in the society and are therefore afraid of organizing. Total amnesty would put them on equal footing with other farm workers. The union opposes guest worker programs.

The strongest antipathy is found among low income U.S. and Canadian citizens. If jobs are lost to refugees or undocumented workers, in the United States it is black, Hispanic and Anglo poor persons who are the main victims, since they are the primary competitors for the same positions. If there is wage depression caused by an oversupply of unskilled labor, these will suffer first and most.

In Canada, the lower the income of the survey respondent, the more immigrants were seen to be a threat to jobs. Eighty-four percent of this group—those who are most likely to be trapped in the recession—thought that jobs for Canadians were being threatened by immigrants. The United Church paper states it well:

"Workers in low-paid jobs with few skills are mostly unorganized and subject to frequent lay-offs. The immigrant becomes a very real threat. Those workers that are most expendable feel the pressure most directly. Immigrants, rather than the actual job situation, become the focus of their anger and concern."

Increased unemployment and economic deprivation in the black community could lead to urban violence, especially where such circumstances are seen as partly resulting from competition with refugees or undocumented workers. Such appears to have been the case in the violence that erupted in the Liberty City area of Miami in May 1980. Since it occurred shortly after the "freedom flotilla" of Cuban refugees came to the Miami area, the crisis was interpreted widely as being caused by that event. Msgr. Brian Walsh, director of the Catholic Services Bureau in Miami, interpreted it otherwise:

"The influx of Cuban refugees into the Miami area and the effect on the black community . . . is more perceived by people outside than people inside the community. Attention has been focused on it because of the national and international press. Outside visitors who come in for brief visits see some things and then relate it to their own past experience and arrive at certain conclusions . . .

"In fact, I think that black leadership in Miami generally will say that when Anglos in Miami focus on this issue they are making the Cuban a scapegoat for the racism in American society . . . The blacks in Miami would have the problems that they have today if no Cubans had ever arrived and if no refugees had arrived. The purpose of a scapegoat is to transfer guilt, and that's one way of avoiding responsibility on the part of Anglo communities."[6]

Certainly all competition between low income U.S. citizens and the influx of refugees and undocumented workers cannot be dismissed that easily. There are clear-cut instances in particular areas and communities where there is competition for jobs, for housing, for social services, and for the public dollar which may be needed to provide for these. However, those who come seeking refuge and a new beginning in this society must not be made the scapegoats for its problems. The Policy Statement on Immigrants, Refugees and Migrants adopted by the National Council of Churches in May 1981, which could be applied in most developed nations, sets specific goals:

"Ending immigration or refugee resettlement . . . will not automatically produce jobs for the poor. Unemployment is high in some areas where resettlement is low, and low in some areas where resettlement is high . . . yet aware that high unemployment aggravates both real and perceived conflicts related to immigration, NCCC shall:

a. Promote resettlement policies which strengthen local communities rather than add to the burdens of areas marked by high unemployment, all the while taking into account the right to free choice of those being resettled;

b. Continue and strengthen its efforts on behalf of the poor and oppressed citizens and residents of the United States;

c. Continue to work for a decent wage for all laborers—citizens, residents, immigrants, refugees and migrants alike—and for the elimination of exploitative employment which encourages unfair competition;

d. Work for legislation which would extend to all foreign migrants and temporary workers employed in the United States full and equal protection of their human rights, and such labor rights as collective bargaining, occupational safety and health, and wage and pension protection; . . .

e. Renew its commitment to work for the establishment of just economic structures which would protect the rights of all United States' citizens and residents to full employment and needed human services . . . "

"We believe a population policy
to be a plan for actions to put people first, in all things.
and to help all people
to be ever more in charge of their own lives.
Just as the riches of the world are for all, not just some,
so all, not just some, are to have a hand
in building a new world social and economic order
that today's four billion persons on earth
are but a pale foreshadowing of what will face
most of tomorrow's some seven billion
if we don't make it our policy now
to put people ahead of profit or any other earthly values . . .

> "Slowly it is being recognized, therefore,
> that it is illogical, futile, cruel and immoral to try to control
> human numbers
> but not change the attitudes, activities and structures
> that surround people and shape what they do about their lives.
> —"What Canadian Population Policy?" excerpted from the ICPOP Working Paper for the Great Canadian Debate about Population and Immigration

Look seriously at the situation of ethnic minorities in your own community. How can churches express Christian compassion and justice on behalf of ethnic minorities, refugees, immigrants and migrants? Can these ministries be viewed within one context?

WHAT CAN CHURCHES DO?

Look at the faces of persons in the migratory streams between Mexico and the United States . . . on the flimsy boats and in the detention camps of fleeing Haitians . . . of the desperate men and women searching for new chances in new places . . .

Christians are struck by the extent of the need and the magnitude of the suffering, angered by the vulnerability to abuse, exploitation and injustice found in the lives of these displaced persons.

How can Christ's church be faithful in responding to the needs and hopes of these "neighbors"? Some of the most creative efforts are taking place at the local level.

—The Center de Asunto Migratories (CAM) in National City, Calif., is an ecumenically supported center which provides counseling for low-income people, especially the undocumented. Through the support of six churches in the San Diego area, the center enables undocumented workers and their families to find their way through the maze of immigration proceedings, with the hope of families being reunited in the United States. The center is also involved in community education and in advocacy work for more just immigration laws.

—The Trinity Coalition in El Paso, Tex., offers a wide range of social services to the immigrant community in the area of Trinity Congregational Church. Five church groups work together to provide day care, family counseling, a home chore service, and a program for family reunification. The Family Reunification Program, cosponsored by the El Paso Community College and by the U.S. Catholic Conference on Immigration, includes immigration counseling, job training and language training.

—The Interfaith Coalition for Justice to Immigrants in Chicago is composed of individuals and organizations who pool their professional or volunteer time to work together on issues that affect immigrant communities. Members of the coalition are organized into work committees addressing different immigrant needs—education in the community, monitoring the local Immigration and Naturalization Service, working against local police abuse of migrants, alerting constituency about developments that affect undocumented persons.

—In the Liberty City area of Miami, the resident U.S. blacks whose sons and daughters already suffer the city's greatest unemployment, are now reaching out to the new people from Haiti. At the Church of the Open Door, a group of volunteer tutors teach basic English to the newcomers as well as help them through the confusion of the new world around them.

There are also a variety of responses which national church organizations can make.

—The American Friends Service Committee uses a community organizing approach in its response to issues along the Mexican-U.S. border. AFSC community organizers serve as consultants to community groups, offering technical and legal assistance. They provide research toward helping people develop their own effective organizations. Their work has been particularly effective among the young women employed by U.S. corporations who have built plants just across the border in Mexico, in order to take advantage of cheap labor.

—The United Methodist Church conducted a "Consulta Fronteriza," Southwestern Border Consultation, in January 1980. The groundwork was laid for new initiatives in church-sponsored human services along the border, in cooperation with the Methodist Church of Mexico. Out of this came the production of a dramatic filmstrip about the Texas-Mexican border, entitled *Borderland,* an effective educational tool for churches of any denomination.

—The General Synod of the United Church of Christ in 1979 and the Lutheran Council in the USA in May 1981 adopted statements on Immigration and the Undocumented Worker.

—The Haitian Refugee Project, based in Washington, D.C., and supported by national church agencies, provides guidance for advocacy regarding the complex issues surrounding the Haitian refugee situation.

What can churches do? When all is said and done, nothing is more important than changing the way that Christians see their neighbors.

Persons without work are also without shelter, food, clothing and medical care. Or they are dependent upon others through government or private channels. For the jobless persons, roots mean work, a steady income.

"Neighbor" then is providing just opportunities to work, the possibility of new starts, the community needed to grow new roots.

Photo by Ray Solowinski

Homeless woman searches through New York City garbage can for food.

Chapter Six:
Being Uprooted In A
Well-Rooted Society

The word "roots" in the Gospels form a fascinating pattern:

—John the Baptist, addressing the religious and political leaders of his day, tells them "The axe is laid to the root of the trees; every tree that does not bear good fruit is cut down and thrown into the fire." (Matt. 3:10; Luke 3:9)

—Jesus, in the parable of the sower, speaks of the seed that fell on rocky ground: "Since it had no root, it withered away." (Matt. 13:6; Mark 4:6) Later, he interprets the parable to refer to those who have "no root in themselves" and who hear the word with joy, but who can't take tribulation or persecution. (Matt. 13:21; Mark 4:17; Luke 8:13)

—In the parable of the wheat and tares, the householder instructs the servants not to gather the tares, lest in doing so they "root up the wheat." God's own judgment time will come. (Matt. 13:29)

Soon afterward, following an encounter with the Pharisees, Jesus says, "Every plant which my heavenly Father has not planted will be rooted up." (Matt. 16:13)

—Following his entry into Jerusalem and on the eve of his final encounter with the religious and political leadership of his day, Jesus curses a fruitless fig tree and it is withered away to its roots. (Mark 11:20) Peter is astonished at the destructive power of Jesus' word. But Jesus' response calls him back to faith in the creative power of God, who can remove mountains and do the impossible.

> Think about this series of passages in light of the power structures of Jesus' day. Then consider what significance these passages may have for power structures in this day. Who really are the "rooted" and the "uprooted" in this time?

Look around the world at uprooted persons—refugees, landless persons, jobless persons. In particular places, these kinds of uprootedness reach into North American society. New immigrants have entered the United States and Canada.

Rural people have lost their land. Undocumented workers have come and some have felt jobs were threatened by these newcomers. Most communities in the United States and Canada can identify these as uprooted persons in their midst.

This does not begin to exhaust the list. It is time now to look intentionally at North American society. Uprootedness is a reality in several major areas of common life. It is time to seek to understand the causes and to ask what is the mission of the church in such circumstances.

WHEN THE FACTORY CLOSES

The voice is that of Don Hardy, a 32-year-old ship fitter at Sun Shipbuilding Company in Chester, just south of Philadelphia. His is one of 3,000 jobs to be lost as this plant closes.

"The politicians have come up empty. And the company, for all its talk about its concern for its employees, is really concerned about getting the work out and closing down their operation. And the union seems unable to come up with anything. So the institutions that workers have had some degree of faith in over the past number of years have basically come up empty."[1]

Philadelphia illustrates a national problem. In the past decade the city has lost 140,000 manufacturing jobs. Some went to the suburbs. But most left the region altogether. The same thing was happening in Baltimore, New York, Boston, Cleveland and Detroit. Job loss hit the Sunbelt as well. In Los Angeles thousands of automobile workers were laid off.

In Sudbury, Ontario, the huge International Nickel Company (INCO) layed off 1,261 hourly rated employees. Another 235 had opted for early retirement, 270 had resigned and 36 had already shifted to another INCO plant.

The prospects of finding new jobs in Sudbury are slim. Many will have to move elsewhere. Marc Lalonde, 22, was one of them. "You can't find a job around here," he says. "You pretty well have to pack up and leave." A local taxi driver says he had taken about 100 young miners to the airport during the two months after the layoff. They were heading for Alberta. The closing was a devastating blow not only to the families but to the local economy.

All this has remained a largely silent tragedy because plants close one-by-one. Families lose their principle source of income, one-by-one. Working class neighborhoods deteriorate, one-by-one. As nations the United States and Canada have not decided what if anything can be done about it.

A factory closing is a traumatic experience in the life of a community. For every 1,000 industrial jobs lost, another 2,000 satellite jobs also have to close—mom and pop stores, restaurants and barber shops.

Some U.S. public officials suggest to blue collar workers that they should "follow the jobs South." Indeed, a U.S. Presidential Commission on National Agenda for the '80s stated that "cities are not permanent" and advises a federal policy that abandons place-oriented programs, saying, "Localities have proved very difficult to shore up." They favored retraining individuals for different work in a new location.

This advice ignores the fact that these workers are individuals who have values which do not travel well. They are attached to extended families, to neighborhoods where several generations live near each other and depend upon one another, to lifetime friends and to churches and schools tested and made familiar over the years. When their factories close, most workers try to stay and take less secure jobs at a lower wage. It is a losing battle and sooner or later either they or their children will have to pull up roots and attempt to start over again.

Not only are people being undermined and humiliated but so is the work ethic in which the United States and Canada have prided themselves.

When sons and daughters see their fathers put out of a job after 20 or 30 years with the same company, their response is no longer to believe that it pays to be loyal, to be diligent, to "put out an honest day's work for an honest day's pay."

One of the factories closing in the Philadelphia area is a multinational corporation's fork lift plant, where 420 jobs will be lost. The corporation will continue making its same product elsewhere—including Japan and Mexico. The corporation had bought out this plant from a local company some years ago. A worker comments, "Yale and Towne was a community company; the community built around it. The conglomerate came in and what they called 'merged' . . . They purged every Yale and Towne officer that had anything to do with that particular plant. They have no feeling for our community."

The corporation holds $2 billion in assets, made a profit of

$116 million in 1980 and owns 156 factories overseas. From his office atop the huge world headquarters of the corporation, an executive comments: "As for Mexico, their government raised the percentage of product foreign companies have to make in Mexico if you want to sell your product there. Japan can make forklift trucks cheaper than the United States. They have a better cost structure. The choice is not between manufacturing fork lifts in Japan or Philadelphia. It is between manufacturing in Japan or not manufacturing at all."

However, Rep. Patrick Dougherty, a conservative Republican from northeast Philadelphia, declares: "We have a skilled work force. But if we don't use it, we will have lost it. Without this force, you bury yourself. We have got to stop these multinationals from running overseas and leaving American workers behind!"

Persons uprooted from lifelong jobs lose not only their livelihood but their identity within the working community. They may also lose their self-respect, their family, and their ability to contribute to community life. There are predictable increases in alcoholism, wife and child abuse, chronic depression, stress and heart attack, admissions to mental hospitals and prison, and suicide.

In Glace Bay, Nova Scotia several jobless people have been driven to suicide. A Canadian church publication reports that one man drove his car into the bay. Another shot himself, leaving a note describing the hopelessness he felt when looking for work.

"The government is trying to make the unemployed feel guilty, shabby and second class," says Peter Giles, one of 6,000 out of work in Sault Ste. Marie. "They think we'll disappear into an abyss of despair—out of sight and out of mind." Giles says that too often people are told "your neighbor is a rotten, lousy, unemployed person who won't work and you are keeping him. To blame us and use a tiny fraction of the truth is a dishonest tactic—evading the issue and evading finding solutions."

Meanwhile, both of the U.S. and Canadian governments are cutting their budgets. The present U.S. administration has made increasingly deep cut in expenditures for social services—just as these services become hard pressed to respond to increased blue collar unemployment. The city of Chester, the 14th most depressed city in the country, already has had its tax base deeply eroded. It struggles to deal with unemployed blue collar workers. Social service budgets are ominously doomed to be far too little to meet the increased need. Experts predict that "the Chester phenomenon" will soon be spreading.

In Canada, some church leaders complain that the government has responded to cries for constraint in spending with cutbacks in social and cultural expenditures, by firing civil servants, and by taking a hard line with trade unions and community groups. "The problem for us is not with the need for restraint in government and elsewhere, but with the priorities of government cuts that cost jobs at a time of high unemployment and at the same time leaves intact massive 'investments' in war planes," says the United Church of Canada working group on social issues.

Glenn Shreffler, a veteran employee of the multinational corporation in Philadelphia, who will soon be jobless, summarizes, "It's profits over people. The company will use the community as long as they can; but then the help has to stop so that they can realize more and more profits. They abandon the community."

WHEN HOUSING RUNS OUT

The South Bronx is described as "probably the worst slum in New York, and, just possibly, the worst in the United States." It covers four square miles just north of Manhattan. Dial Torgerson of the *Los Angeles Times* described the South Bronx:

"By every yardstick of distress, it is the 'urb' least likely to succeed. It has 136 kid gangs, with 10,000 members; 20,000 addicts; 40 percent of the population gets welfare; it has the highest crime rate of all New York.

"Between structures still standing are vacant lots covered with rubble, where structures were vandalized, burned, then destroyed as dangerous. The population is dwindling, as buildings are abandoned, but those who remain suffer even greater overcrowding, meaning less space, more tension, less chance to get the garbage picked up, more rats, more cockroaches, more disease.

" 'Sal si Puedes' they say in the South Bronx, 'leave if you can.' Those who can, have. The people who are there are there because there is no place else for them. And yet, amid the agony, life persists.

"Bulldozer urban renewal was halted in the sixties as the poor found a political voice. 'Urban renewal is Negro removal,' the saying went. The clearing of entire districts by governmental agencies is rare, now.

"But the residents of blighted blocks see gaps appearing in the house fronts, year by year, and realize that attrition is achieving the same ends as the dozer blade and the wrecking ball. Because of abandonment and demolition, slum population statistically dwindle as overcrowding grows."[2]

Canada is not without such urban problems. Listen to the story of one Canadian child:

"My name is Pierre and I'm 13 years old. I'm the eldest of seven children. What makes me suffer most is not having a house, having to live in a shack where it's always cold and too small for all the family. There are nine of us. The seven children all sleep together in two 36" wide beds—pushed together in the winter for more heat since we don't have enough blankets. We have an old broken-down stove, but it's dangerous.

"Autumn isn't very much fun either. It's cold also, and the rats come in—you have to watch so they won't bite the smaller children. This week they chewed off part of the pump so we have no water and the neighbors tell us their well is low, so we do without water. We're not always clean when we go to school."[3]

Pierre is from New Brunswick but similar poverty exists in all the provinces. Census reports indicate that more than 1.6 million children in Canada live in similar circumstances.

The presence of such poverty, in the heart of America's cities should not hide the genuine progress made in providing housing. Since World War II , the achievement has been tremendous. Whereas in 1936, one-third of the United States could be described as ill housed, by 1970 the figure had dropped to less than one million. The U.S. national census reported in 1970 that only 15 percent of the country's dwelling units were overcrowded, using the standard of one person per room.

Yet no one who walks the main streets of the South Bronx, the Dorchester section of Boston, East Woodlawn in Chicago or any number of other U.S. and Canadian cities could take much pride in the nations' housing achievements. In the United States the 10 percent of the population who live in substandard housing amounts to approximately 20 million persons.

The statistics do not say how many families will soon be forced to move to substandard housing because their incomes cannot keep pace with climbing rent.

Another sober fact must be considered. The reforms in housing achieved during the past few decades have benefited primarily middle-class working people. Further progress will need to benefit the struggling poor persons of the United States and Canada—at an apparent cost to the power, the comfort and, possibly, the safety of the middle class. The high correlation between bad housing, low income, and membership in a minority group carries with it an unmistakable political message. Poor persons may have to take desperate actions as they can no longer expect to obtain better, or even adequate, housing from a general drive to improve housing standards for the middle class.

"Urban renewal" which uprooted many in the sixties is no longer being carried out in a bulldozer manner. However, a new phenomenon has taken its place, the "gentrification" of the inner city. The city is becoming an increasingly fashionable place to live for young, affluent professional "20th century gentry." Once again poor persons are being ripped up by their roots to make room for these new residents.

The building and renovation of houses in the inner city has become a very profitable industry. Rent increases of 300 percent and more and sales realizing as much as 1,000 percent profit have been documented. Gentrification in many cities has caused great racial unrest and urban tension. Many social observers predict that the disinherited, uprooted inner-city nomads will become a major social problem in the 1980s. Instead of the poor having their housing needs seriously addressed, they are again the pawns in a game for those with money.

Shortly after Hurricane Camille struck the southern United States in 1969, New York City's former housing and development administrator said:

"When a Hurricane Camille strikes and leaves 4,000 or 5,000 families without homes, the nation's attention is galvanized. The Federal Government responds with crisis aid, declarations of emergency are issued, the National Guard is thrown into action. Yet in our cities a thousand times that number of families are ill-housed, virtually homeless. But because they are the victims of a slow, creeping process rather than a sudden catastrophe, we as a nation are neither excited nor galvanized into action, even though the emergency, the crisis, the disaster is more real than 10 Camilles.''[4]

Consider your area. What is happening to housing in the inner city? Has there been urban renewal? Gentrification? What has been the effect on poor persons? Has there been any effort toward improvement of housing in rural areas? What can the church do to bring about appropriate action by government and the housing industry?

WHEN HOME DISINTEGRATES

Factory closings and housing shortages are only two of the external factors which help to create uprootedness in communities. Internal factors are happening with this society to tear people up by the roots and thrust them out to an unknown destiny.

The stresses and pressures upon the home are known to all. The extended family is almost a relic of the past. The nuclear family unit must cope with a society that often seems too much to handle. The highly competitive economic system creates anxiety about "success" and, for many, survival. The strong emphasis on individual fulfillment and satisfaction places constant strain on relationships. Rapid technological and social changes make parents strangers in their children's world. It is little wonder that under such stress homes often disintegrates. In fact, it is a wonder that so many homes survive!

The victims of this disintegration are usually women and children, as with today's refugee population. Sometimes it is a temporary but painful displacement. Desertion and divorce, which now ends one marriage in three, leave women suddenly alone and responsible for their own financial security, as well as that of their families. Many have either never been employed or have not held jobs for many years. They face emotional and practical obstacles in establishing independence and putting down roots again. Likewise the disruption of the lives of children of divorced parents, while not insurmountable, is still traumatic.

The disintegration of the home has brought about two groups of "modern North American refugees" that deserve particular attention—battered women and runaway youth.

108

Certainly if Christians are concerned about the world's uprooted persons, they cannot ignore these uprooted who are among them, in every community, in virtually every church.

Battered Women

The problem of battered women has come into the limelight only in the past few years; its progression toward public awareness paralleling the growth of the women's movement. Historically, little public outcry has been heard against this brutality. But it is now evident the problem is far more pervasive—and damaging—than it was ever thought to be. Some observers estimate that as many as 50 percent of all women will be battering victims at some time in their lives. It is impossible to estimate how many of these suffer such physical and psychological abuse as to gain the ignominious title of "battered women."

The whole spectrum of intrafamily violence is only beginning to be given serious study. What is becoming apparent is that there is a relationship between battered women and child abuse. Men who beat women were often themselves beaten as children. There is a high incidence of female child incest in families where there is violence. From television and movie brutality to the glorification of war, the pervasiveness of violence in North American society has taken its toll in the basic unit of society, the nuclear family.

The women's movement has helped to show domestic violence as the outcropping of a latent violence committed by men against women in general. Many of society's institutions have been set up with men responsible for taking care of women, including the family. These male dominated institutions are unresponsive to the female victims of their own aggressiveness. Sexism becomes the hidden cause of much human suffering. Men fight with other men to prove they are not "sissies" like women. Men beat women in order to fulfill a socialized need to maintain dominance. Women show passive faces to the world for fear of hurting men's masculine self-image. Hence the struggle for more equal power relationships between men and women is really a struggle for a more just, equitable and harmonious society.

For most battered women, leaving home is the action of last resort. Stories abound of women who have sustained years and years of nearly constant physical violence because they "didn't know where to go." Lack of alternative shelter and financial resources have kept battered women in a "learned helplessness" while enduring abusive, life-threatening situations. As shelters and other services have become more numerous and accessible in the past few years, vast numbers of women are acknowledging their victimization and making decisions to change their lives.

Now that the brutal reality is becoming known, congressional committees, civil rights commissions, and other government agencies are studying the problem. Laws to protect battered women are being introduced in legislatures in most states. Concerned community groups are lobbying to gain adequate funding and services, including "safe houses," legal and medical help, crisis intervention and therapy services. Of course, the long-range task is one which involves everyone— eliminating sex role stereotyping during child development, reducing violence in society, reducing the harshness in child discipline, understanding the rightful role of women in home and society.[5]

Running Away

In vastly increasing numbers, young people are running away from home "to cut the ties that hurt." The reasons range from the desperate to the sublime—they run to hide, to escape, to forget, to follow a dream, to make a new beginning. Regardless of the reason, taking such a leave is a cry of pain that life as they have known it is no longer tolerable.

The National Network of Runaways and Youth Services estimates that some 1.8 million children in the United States "disappear" each year. Some are the victims of parental kidnappings. Others are the victims of foul play. But most are runaways. So common an occurrence has it become that less than 10 percent are entered in the FBI's missing persons file. Not nearly as high as the percentage of stolen cars reported! The average age of runaways for the past several years has been 15. At least half are girls.

Youth run from a wide variety of "brutal realities." Some flee a home torn by divorce or desertion. They may blame themselves for the separation. If a choice between parents is involved, they may be ambivalent, perhaps identifying with both and resenting that a choice must be made at all. They may try to ease the anxiety by running from one parent to the other or by starting out on a search for their own identity apart from home and parents.

Many teenagers run away to rid themselves of drinking parents. Alcoholism, the ignored American disease, affects from 6.5 to 9 million adults, and its agony is fast being transmitted to their children. In concentrating on the personal torment of the alcoholic, it is easy to forget his or her children and the suffering caused to them by the habit.

Departure sometimes signifies disappointment with life in general, as well as with themselves. Parents do not understand. They are unrealistically harsh in their rules or expectations. There is a brother or sister who is impossible. There is fear of recrimination for poor school grades. A recurring theme in this generation is that youth leave the "hypocrisy" of their household or society, going in search of warmth, integrity, and meaning which they have been led to believe thrive within counter-culture communities.

Most runaways return within a week. "The city was lonely." "There was no place to stay, nothing to do." "The money ran out." Sometimes their action opens a long-closed door to communication with parents. Their one-time fling may lead them to a deepened appreciation for the home which at one time seemed intolerable.

But it is the desperate and the determined who are really rootless. Shunning conventional society, they view any established agency with suspicion. The attitude is often reciprocal. They are nobody's children and theirs is the last juvenile problem to be considered by already burdened agencies.

Yet for many the freedom which they sought becomes slavery. This is particularly true for those who gravitate to the large cities. New York, for example, has an estimated 20,000 under-16 runaways, and thousands more between 16 and 21.

"They aren't bad kids," says Father Bruce Ritter, director of the "Under-21" Crisis Center and Sanctuary near Times Square in New York City. "Most have run away from parents or guardians who abused them, or they're throwaways whose parents kicked them out. They come to New York because it's a big city and they think they'll be able to find new lives here. Most are unemployable. Pimps pick them up, sweet-talk them, feed and give them lodging—then beat, rape, exploit, torture and even kill them. In one three-year period, 176 prostitutes, including many kids, have been murdered. But that doesn't include suicides and the ones who were given drug overdoses. You want some troublesome kid dead, you OD him. Who cares?"[6]

Fortunately, efforts are underway in almost every major city to halt the massive destruction of the runaway children by those who would exploit them. Hotlines give them a chance to get in touch with parents or trusted friends who may be of help to them. Halfway houses are available to feed, clothe, shelter and care for those who come. Free clinics treat their many medical needs—malnutrition, hepatitis, tuberculosis, mononucleosis, drug-related problems and the various forms of venereal disease. Youth centers offer counseling as well as informal advice-giving from contemporaries.

Yet there is much need for a "shot of love" to be given to these modern refugees, to assure them that they are respected as human beings and that their lives have value. Bridge-building is desperately needed between them and the generation which they have fled. Clearly regardless of the pace or degree of change, human beings desperately need one another.[7]

WHEN THERE'S NO PLACE LEFT CALLED HOME

"I lost my job, lost my lady—everything just hit me at the same time. That's how I wound up with no place to stay. That's why I'm here." Ricky Bernard Beulah, a 25-year-old black man, drew on a cigarette and shook his head. "That was nine months ago. Seven years—I mean in love, married, two kids. She got another job and another man, too, so this is what it's come to." He motioned towards the church gymnasium, his home for the night.

A native of Atlanta, Beulah is one of the young black males who swell the city's unemployment rolls. He is a high school graduate and a "jack of all trades" who is more than willing to work. But he cannot find a job.

"I do construction work, warehouse work—anything. I just need a job, an opportunity to work. I wanna work. But there ain't no work out there. I fill out applications all the time."

He stood there without shoes, bearded, shirt open, bare chested, wearing blue jeans, looking into the distance. At length he said, "I hope your story makes the businessman give the po' man a job. That's what he needs."[8]

Ricky Bernard Beulah is one of a swelling number of urban

refugees, otherwise called "the homeless," "street people," "the down and out." On each winter night in 1981-82 in Atlanta, an estimated 1,500 to 2,000 persons have no fixed address and no money for shelter. The figures represent a 50 percent increase over the previous winter.

Atlanta is only one of many U.S. and Canadian cities with streets that are heavy with homeless persons.

"You always have homeless people; this year we have more," said Joanna Adams, community minister of Central Presbyterian Church, Atlanta, and the person in charge of the church's hospitality program for the homeless. "There are more this year because the economy has finally caught up with those who were just hanging on by their fingernails. They've finally fallen through the slats of society."

Atlanta's homeless in the winter of 1981-82 are fairly representative of the homeless found in other American cities, estimated conservatively at a quarter of a million in the United States alone. About 90 percent are men; about 10 percent are women and children. They range from the late teens to the elderly. They fall into three major groups: the chronically mentally ill, the victims of alcohol or drugs, and the new breed of homeless, those who are simply unable to find work and a place to live.

Among the 36,000 homeless in New York City, an estimated 50 to 60 percent are the mentally ill who have been "deinstitutionalized," released from mental hospitals. For a variety of reasons, state mental hospitals have discharged approximately a quarter of a million mentally ill and retarded people in the last decade. Since 1965, for example, the population of New York state mental hospitals has dropped from 85,000 to 23,000. In theory, the patients were expected to benefit from a return to the community. In practice, however, many were victims of "poor discharge planning." They have been left to roam at will without family or friends, without regular income and without stable, supportive places to live.

Some other street people, though never hospitalized on a long-term basis, are no less emotionally disturbed. "Just living on the street can create mental disorientation," say Ellen Baxter, coauthor of a study of the homeless done by New York's Community Service Society. "Lack of sleep, lack of food, being assaulted continuously—these are factors."

In the 1960s, the "dewarehousing" of the mentally ill

through the use of newly-discovered control drugs was applauded as humane and liberal. Today it is recognized as one of society's most serious problems. Not that the idea is a bad one. Rather, that so little was done to prepare for their reentry into society.

But a growing number of the homeless are people walking the streets simply because they are without jobs. Most are young, 18 to 25. Many are black or Hispanic. More and more, entire families are living in their cars, traveling in search of work until the end of their gas money dictates where they stop. Some sleep in abandoned buildings, others in bus and train stations, still others under bridges and in doorways. Their days are spent in endless walking, searching for a job, for a break from the wind, a place to sit, or simply somewhere to urinate.

What is the situation of the homeless in your town or city? Whose responsibility should it be to provide some sort of basic shelter and food for them? The city? The nation? The church? What long-range prospects are there for the "new breed of homeless" who simply can't find work?

WHEN THERE'S NO ONE LEFT WHO CARES

Julia didn't see or hear too well, which was probably a blessing. Wanting to be hospitable, she raised her arm and pointed to a faded photograph of herself and her family. She, young and plump at 21. Around her neck was a silver crucifix. "I am High Episcopalian. I was christened in Camden on June 28, 1899. There's no one left but me," she said sadly, "so I know God left me here for some purpose."

"Do you get much food? Does anyone go to the store for you?" I asked, seeing how thin she was.

Her voice cracked. "No, there ain't been nobody around at all."

Once, on a Saturday, she had tried to go to a local supermarket, but she tripped and fell in the gutter. She lay there for a long time before a little boy stopped and helped her. She tried once again, on a Tuesday. That time she got to the store and managed to buy a few things, but on the way home someone grabbed the bag of groceries and ran away. After that she was simply afraid to try, so she sat there in her torn green chair among the roaches, waiting for the guests who never arrived, and waiting also, rather patiently, for God to let her know the special role that God had in mind for her.[9]

Julia, like many of her elderly neighbors, lives in a two-room shack in a little alley in South Philadelphia. Often the shacks are without heat or water or gas or food.

In order to reach the city's hungry senior citizens, the Philadelphia Corporation for Aging established 13 feeding centers throughout Philadelphia. The centers were so over-crowded on opening day that most were forced to turn people away. A food supply designed to take care of 100 people fed 200. The "nutritional supplement" amounted to only one-sixth of the adult minimum daily requirement. But it was better than nothing, so they came. Some brought jars in which to place a part of their meager meal, so that night at least they would have dinner.

Housing for the elderly has become a major concern as the average life expectancy increases. Yet in spite of the facilities being developed in the commercial market, by government programs and even by churches, there is a growing segment of the elderly in the United States and Canada who are finding themselves in the same plight as Julia. Their pensions and retirement incomes simply no longer can meet their basic needs. When there is no one left who cares, they may spend the last years of their lives alone in some apartment or hovel, isolated and unseen by the world around them, hungry for food and for human compassion. They are among the most pitiful of the world's uprooted persons.

What is the situation regarding housing for the elderly in your community? Is there provison for low-income senior citizens? What kind of ministries are there that reach into their lives?

WHAT CAN THE CHURCHES DO?

The story of the world's uprooted people has come close to home. It is evident that uprootedness is indeed a serious crisis in this society. The crisis is difficult to handle for it disturbs the often complacent view of U.S. and Canadian communities. Eyes must open to persons who are usually hidden. Or possibly the uprooted persons are people from whom North American Christians have hidden themselves.

How does the church respond to the uprooted right where it is? Certainly the churches do not have all the answers. The church confronts systemic problems which defy easy solutions. The present upheavals are deep-seated in origin. They call not so much for quick answers as for long-term commitment.

One thing is clear: The poor and powerless people are being pushed, pressured and uprooted by forces which alternately neglect and exploit them. If the church is to stand in the biblical tradition, it must be willing to fulfill its prophetic role on behalf of the poor, being their advocate in the centers of political and economic power.

The people of the United States face a particularly crucial period in their relation to the poor persons in their midst. The Governing Board of the National Council of Churches of Christ expressed the nature of the crisis in a message to the churches adopted in May 1981, entitled "The Remaking of America?" which states in part:

"Since the havoc of the Great Depression, administrations of both parties have recognized an ultimate responsibility in the federal government to promote the conditions in which all members of this society have enough to eat, a decent place to live, a basic education, and the necessities of a minimum standard of living, not as a matter of charity but of entitlement.

"That goal has never been attained but for half a century the nation has been moving toward it—until now. The policy of the new (Reagan) administration is not just to cut back on human services, but to deny that people are entitled to them. By its budget recommendations, which eliminate many human service programs and sharply curtail others, it seeks not to slow the nation's progress toward the goal, but to reverse its commitment. When inflation has rendered the current "poverty level" obsolete, to cut back even farther to a so-called "safety net" for the "truly needy" is to abandon the working poor to hopelessness and destitution, particularly in a time of limited economic growth. It is a turn backward from the effort to build an economic floor for the whole society to a former time when America was officially indifferent to the suffering of those whose best efforts were not enough.

"Such a reversal of America's national commitment to a more humane society is contrary to the best insights of both Christian faith and national creed."

If the church is to fulfill its prophetic role in society today, it must speak up for poor persons in such a time as this, calling governments to take very seriously their responsibility for the general welfare of the people.

"When Christians have lived most fully according to the gospel," says the NCCC Governing Board message, "they have urged the nations toward care and compassion, not away from them. The Scriptures call us to a vision that supercedes all social visions, to a vision of a 'good and broad land,' a new earth and a new heaven . . . . The Christian Church has not always served this vision-above-all-visions well, often more concerned for its own institutional success or survival than for the plight of the poor. In these days, when economic anxiety lures fundamental fears and selfishness to the surface of human motivation and the nation is tempted to make them the basis of policy, we must never forget that 'judgment begins with the household of God.' "

> Respond to the above quotation. What kind of national policy in relation to "the general welfare" should the church advocate?

"One of the devils' neatest (and most successful) tricks is to convince us that a problem is too big—that it would be folly to tackle such a major need with such meager resources. 'Better quit; give up; or better still, don't start!' the devil whispers in our attentive ears. And how often that tactic works, even though we Christians have at our disposal the effective, and proven, economics of Jesus, which expand the small, upon being blessed by God, into gracious plenty."
—Millard Fuller, founder of Habitat for Humanity

The faith of the "economics of Jesus" reflected by Fuller is the kind of faith Christians need individually and corporately to respond to the uprooted persons in their own home towns. Christians are called to participate in "parabolic action," action which may appear minuscule compared to the enormity of the problem, but which serves as a parable pointing toward how society should function in order to move toward the coming of the community of the sovereign God.

Such action may not be immediately successful by the world's standards. Take, for example, the effort of the Ecumenical Coalition of Youngstown, Ohio. U.S. Steel announced on Nov. 19, 1979, the closing of 15 of its facilities, including two mills in Youngstown, which would eliminate an estimated 13,000 jobs.

The Ecumenical Commission first presented a resolution to U.S. Steel requesting the Board of Directors prepare and make public a report describing the social and economic impact of the closing on employees and communities, the number of jobs lost and resulting tax loss to local government, and what actions the corporation planned to take as part of its responsibility to employees and community.

Going still further, the commission developed a plan for the purchase of one of the factories by the workers themselves, in order that the factory not only could stay open but also so that it might express a new kind of worker controlled management which would give priority to people. Due to lack of sufficient capital the experiment failed. Yet, the effort pointed toward a more humane way for an industrial society to operate.

Quite a number of churches and church agencies have made a valiant effort to respond to the needs of poor persons for housing. This will become increasingly difficult with the cuts in federal loans for low cost housing.

In the early '70s the congregation of Parkdale United in Toronto faced a $500,000 bill to restore its nearly century-old church. The church had been built to serve the middle and upper class neighborhood that had surrounded it. Those people are gone now. The neighborhood is low income, many working poor persons, trapped in poor housing.

The old church was torn down and in its place the congregation built an apartment building for low income working single persons. The 11-story building provides attractive studio apartments for persons with an income below $12,000. The rent is much lower than similar housing in the area. The land was donated by the church and a foundation runs the building. The church rents its space. A small, inviting chapel on the first floor serves the congregation.

Habitat for Humanity is another especially challenging example. Stating its purpose as providing "a decent house in a decent community for God's people in need," it began its efforts in the heart of rural southwest Georgia. The desperate state of housing among poor families in rural areas, particularly black families, brought deep concern to the residents of Koinonia, an integrated Christian experiment in community living.

118

In 1969, after much discussion and prayer, they launched into the task of building 42 homes, replacing flimsy shacks with solid dwellings. Houses were sold at cost with a small down payment, the purchasers carrying a 20-year, no-interest mortgage.

From the beginning, the movement has mushroomed. Now not only are new houses being built at the rate of one every two or three weeks in the area of Americus, but projects have been organized and house construction is underway in 14 other low-income communities across the country, especially in the rural South. Indeed, the dream has expanded abroad and projects have been started in Zaire, Guatemala, Uganda and Haiti. The philosophy of Habitat for Humanity, according to Fuller, is "that the economically poor need capital, not charity; coworkers, not caseworkers. They need partners; people who love and respect them and who want to stand beside them and help free them of the burdens they bear."

Sometimes the parabolic action called for is not so much in brick and mortar as in providing a refuge for those uprooted by disintegration of the family. Several of the ministries related to the Office of Ministries with Women in Crisis of the United Methodist Church are beautiful examples:

—The Door Opener in Mason City, Iowa, provided four drop-in centers for women who are feeling the impact of personal crisis. Displaced homemakers are of special concern. They are helped to identify skills and expand them through training and career assessment programs. A crisis line is available for victims of domestic violence, rape and incest, with volunteers trained to provide shelter, transportation and support.

—The N.E.W.S. Shelter for Battered Women in Kanas City, Mo., is one of the most inclusive shelters in existence in relation to race and class. Located in the heart of Kansas City's urban neighborhood, the Shelter offers a unique educational ministry to area churches. It has a high rate of success in placing women in low-income housing in the immediate neighborhood so that long-term follow-through with women and children is possible. A program for men who batter is in the initial stages.

Similarly, church-related ministries for runaway youths— halfway houses, free clinics, youth counseling centers—express the effort to build a bridge into the world of these who have uprooted themselves from home and family.

Where is there greater need for parabolic action than in the response of the church to those who literally have no home? In Atlanta, the 35-member congregation of Clifton Presbyterian Church was the first to respond to the critical need of the street people for a night refuge from the winter cold. Its courageous action pricked the conscience of the entire Christian community in the city.

Now five large downtown Atlanta churches open their facilties each night during the winter to provide warmth and safety. Congregations across the metropolitan area participate in providing simple meals and volunteers to staff the hospitality centers. "Our ugly old gymnasium that is used for the hospitality centers has become a sanctuary," say Joanna Adams, "a sanctuary where people are being saved—not only the street people, but those who come to serve."

Thus in many diverse ways in the modern world of the uprooted which crowds in upon each town, Christians are responding to the New Testament call to "show hospitality." Henry Nouwen captures the spirit of that ancient exhortation:

"Hospitality means primarily the creation of a free space where the stranger can enter and become a friend instead of an enemy. Hospitality is not to change people, but to offer them a place where change can take place. It is not to bring men and women over to our side, but to offer freedom not disturbed by dividing lines. It is not to lead our neighbor into a corner where there are no alternatives left, but to open a wide spectrum of options for choice and commitment. It is the liberation of fearful hearts so that words can find roots and bear ample fruit. It is the opening of that opportunity to others to find their God and their way."

Chapter Seven:
Building A Whole Community

Abraham and Sarah were sojourners, strangers living on somebody else's land. Even David, the ideal king of Israel, in his moments of deepest spiritual insight, had a sense of being a stranger and a sojourner on the earth. (1 Chron. 29:14-15)

The early Christians out of painful experience recaptured this spirit. They were persecuted and scattered. (Acts 8:1) They lived as exiles and aliens in strange lands. (1 Pet. 1:1, 17; 2:11) Yet, in their uprootedness, they had found new roots in Christ. (Col. 2:7; Eph. 3:17) In their relation to God, they were no longer strangers and sojourners. They were citizens of the household of God. (Eph. 2:19)

The passage which probably expresses this spirit most clearly is Hebrews 11:1 through 12:3. This "hall of fame" of people of faith culminates in Jesus, "the pioneer and perfecter of our faith." Look especially at Hebrews 11:13-16.

"These all died in faith, not having received what was promised, but having seen it and greeted it from afar, and having acknowledged that they were strangers and exiles on the earth. For people who speak thus make it clear that they are seeking a homeland. If they had been thinking of that land from which they had gone out, they would have had opportunity to return. As it is, they desire a better country, that is, a heavenly one. Therefore God is not ashamed to be called their God, for God has prepared for them a city."

Read verse 13 in several translations. In the latter part of the verse, the first term is almost consistently translated "strangers," but the second term is variously translated "pilgrims" (KJV), "exiles" (RSV), "passing travelers" (NEB) and "refugees" (TEV).

What does this verse say to Christians about their attitude toward life in this world?

Calvin put it: "But we know that if we shall be banished from one country, the whole world is the Lord's; and that if we be thrown out of the world itself, nevertheless we shall not be altogether outside of his kingdom."[1]

121

A modern interpreter, Roy I. Sano, expresses it this way: "We are not called to create settlers, but sojourners . . . In a day of accelerated changes, when evils of our past have become so conspicuous, the people of God in this land cannot become settlers who sanction or sanctify the status quo. We need sojourners who, "having acknowledged that they are strangers and exiles on the earth . . . look forward to the city which has foundations, whose builder and maker is God."[2]

Think about this simple interpretation of the Hebrews passage: "Home is not back there, but out front."

The final question asked in meeting persons who have been uprooted has been "What can the churches do?" The range of possible responses is vast, and calls for the commitment of the church from the local to the national and international dimensions.

The discussion must not be limited to ways which "we" as settled affluent North American Christians may do good to "them," the world's uprooted persons. As all who are involved in ministry with uprooted persons can testify, there is much to learn and receive.

What can uprooted persons teach those with roots? For persons who claim the name of Christian, the uprooted can help the rooted *rediscover what it means to be "strangers and pilgrims on earth."* Settled Christians face the temptation to flee an ever-changing world, finding false security in possessions, buildings or even in church and religious arenas. The world's uprooted persons show not only that the world will not permit such escape, but that neither will God.

Frederick A. Norwood, toward the close of his history of religious refugees, draws this lesson for the contemporary church:

"Disruption becomes a characteristic of Christian life, individually, socially, spiritually. No refugee can be sure of what the morrow holds: insecurity, anxiety, frustration, and fear are woven into the fabric of life . . . Does this suggest that the church in the world must be prepared to be scattered, to lose its institutional roots, the accouterments of its visible form? Is the entire story of religious refugees over the centuries a sort of prognostication for the church in the world of tomorrow?"[3]

Uprooted persons help their rooted Christian neighbors rediscover the vision of "diaspora Christianity," the church scattered in the world, learning to travel light. The presence of these uprooted persons in the world and the church's deliberate presence with them may enable Christians to form a "supple and lean church," prepared to move out from the status quo at any moment, to non-conform freely. They may enable Christians to rediscover that the church's essential being is always in the process of becoming.

> Looking at your own congregation, to what extent would you describe it as a company of "strangers and pilgrims on the earth"? To what extent is it "conformed to the world" and to what extent "transformed by a complete change of mind"? (Rom. 12:2) Would you dare to ask for such an evaluation of your congregation from a refugee? An undocumented person? A runaway youth? A street person?

The world's uprooted persons also remind Christians that, *whatever the present apparent security, "we're all in the same boat."* David James Randolph preached a sermon on this theme at Christ Church, Manhattan, drawing on the imagery of Jesus with the disciples in a storm at sea. (Matt. 8:23-27) Randolph spoke of the common experience which comes to all who "find ourselves in a storm at sea, to find ourselves troubled, to find the lifeboat in which we are traveling across the sea of life threatened."

Sometimes insecurity may be relatively minor and temporary; sometimes life itself is at stake. When Christians see pictures of uprooted persons "spilling over international waters all over the globe," fleeing for their lives and chasing the dream of a better life, Christians can remember that "we're all in the same boat." Caught in the storm, Christians, like the disciples cry out, "Save us, Lord! We are perishing!" To calm fears as well as to calm the sea, Christians turn to the God who is in the same boat with them. They turn to Christ who shares the storm.

Certainly in this contemporary interdependent world, Christians are in the same boat with the world's uprooted people.

In a world where marching armies have been made obsolete by intercontinental ballistic missiles, the apparent security of the North American continent between two wide oceans is an illusion. This continent is one of the prime targets for the most destructive forces which human beings ever created.

Should the unthinkable happen, where would those who

survive flee for refuge? Similarly, within this society, the economic and social forces which are at work creating uprootedness may well reach into the apparent security of any one community, any neighborhood, any household. Should that happen, would there be a place to turn for help? The presence of uprooted persons among the rooted and the presence of the rooted with those seeking refuge continually reminds, *It can happen here.*

What factors do you see in the life of the nation and the world which threaten to place you among the world's uprooted? How can you help avert such an eventuality? What would you do if it occurred?

But there is a more positive lesson to be learned. *The uprooted persons bring contributions which can enrich the whole community's life.* While at present the uprooted persons may have desperate needs, they also bring particular skills, distinctive cultures, and individual spiritual gifts. The perspective of faith recognizes that divine grace is at work in all lives, even in the middle of inhumanity, indignities, and atrocities which may spread across the human story. Christians must not allow service to others to blind them to the work which God has done and is doing in, through and with the whole human community. Settled, affluent Christians must be open to receive what God has to offer through others.

While this lesson needs to be learned by each person individually, it also needs to be learned by whole nations. The United States once proudly called itself the melting pot for peoples of all nations. It has now become more and more resistant to the entry of those who may bring a different culture or religion or political orientation into the mix. However, no longer can North Americans see their national identity as fixed and static. Not only because the turbulent, interrelated world won't permit it, but because North American citizens deprive themselves of the richness of the variety of the world's peoples by attempting to preserve things as they are.

The predominantly white, Anglo-Saxon, Protestant identity of the United States and Canada has no guarantee of continuing in perpetuity. The growing number of non-white ethnic minorities, who after all are the majorities in the world as a whole, come as immigrants, refugees and migrants. These sojourners and strangers are not to be viewed as invading bar-

barians who have broken through frontier barriers and threaten to pollute imagined purity. Rather, they come bringing gifts which can increase still further the many splendored variety of the earth's peoples who share visions of a society where many are one. There is unity in diversity, where every human life is seen as precious and makes a contribution to the well-being of the whole.

Sang H. Lee, professor at Princeton Theological Seminary, has expressed concern that there is so little meaningful interaction between the 1,000 Korean immigrant churches and their white counterparts. He speaks of how often the two congregations may use the same building, and yet pass by each other, physically so close but still oceans apart. He calls both sides "to give up some of their ethnocentric security and to immigrate into each other's worlds," to puncture their secure circles of cultural captivity and "to make room for genuine human space for each other."

His quotation from H. Richard Neibuhr can well be a theme which guides in the growing variety of world's people who share a common life: "Through Christ we become as immigrants into the empire of God which extends over all the world and learn to remember the history of that empire, that is of people in all times and places, as our history."[4]

> List the gifts and contribution which can be brought into the life of your nation by some of the uprooted persons who have been mentioned in this study, and by some whom you may know personally. How can you and your congregation better become "immigrants into the empire of God"?

Uprooted persons also *give a deeper understanding of the larger drama taking place in the world*. What God is up to in human history, says Sano, is "the creation of livable space." God calls everyone to participate in this task. Therefore those who work in providing homes for the homeless millions are co-workers with God.

But within that larger drama, forces are at work frustrating God's intention to provide for all a place to live and adequate resources for survival. Consequently, conditions have developed which uproot millions and create unlivable spaces so that people must move or flee elsewhere.

Sano proceeds to analyze the U.S. and Canadian place in this problem. "It has become increasingly clear that our own twin doctrines of increased development and national security, and the agencies which implement them, play key roles." U.S. and Canadian aspirations for economic development send their citizens and businesses abroad in search of raw materials and natural resources for their industries.

Cities mushroom as transplanted farmers and their families come looking for work. Capital-intensive corporate operations replace traditional labor-intensive ones. Thousands of workers become obsolete and must try to find work elsewhere.

In such a cauldron "the contradiction between aspiration and frustration" creates deep unrest and calls forth repressive measures by national leaders, in order that "development" may proceed without disruption. Those who will not comply are arrested without charges, tried by military tribunals, imprisoned without sentence. Such is the making of violations of human rights and the creation of political exiles.

Meanwhile, the task of combatting "international conspiracy and terrorism" proves more than national elites can tackle, so there enter the superpower support systems through intelligence networks and large military assistance and presence.

Reflecting upon this analysis theologically, Sano states: "Our understanding of developmentalism and our definition of national security have elements of a curse for humankind. They are the 'principalities and powers' which control the course of human events. They have usurped the place of God. In place of the reign of God's truth, they permeate societies with the half-truths of consumerism, or peddle outright lies through censorships. Rather than the pervasive compassion we associate with the reign of God's love, they inflict the reign of terror in martial laws and variations of it . . . .

"The central issue is not whether God exists or not, but what is given sacrosanct status and what gods are before us . . . . What we see happening in human history at this juncture of our lives is the dismantling of the reign of these gods. The unrelenting God of biblical faith stirs up people who work for those conditions which restore this earth to livable space."[5]

Reflect upon the various experiences of the world's uprooted which have been presented in this study. For how many of them do you find that Sano's analysis is correct? What is your analysis of the "larger drama" within which this uprooted of millions is taking place?

The world's uprooted persons confront their well-rooted neighbors with the inescapable presence of Christ. Through Matthew 25, Christians see these—the hungry, the thirsty, and the imprisoned—as the embodiment of Christ in this time and place. An openness to them opens the way for a new experience in Christ who waits to give life to those who give life away for others.

The gift received from persons who come from far or near is greater than anything done for them. Pride and power are confounded by them. The powerlessness of uprooted persons gives an opportunity to find a new meaning for salvation. It is as though Jesus appeals through uprooted persons for all to be "reconciled to God."

Yet, strangely at the same time, the settled, affluent, rooted Christian find access to a new kind of power—power to love, to empathize, to endure. It does not offer a solution to every problem or a way around every obstacle. Yet it does teach that the more dared, the more the impossible can happen. The Christians experience the truth which Paul discovered—Christ is "able to be exceeding abundantly above all that we ask or think, according to the power at work in us." (Eph. 3:20)

Pause to think of personal experiences in being with and ministering to uprooted persons which have given you this sense of the presence of Christ. Listen to the testimony of others about such experiences.

Finally, the world's uprooted persons *renew in all hearts the hope and the vision of the community of the sovereign God.* Uprooted persons left without power and protection, live by hope—hope sometimes rooted in God and God's ultimate justice and grace, hope sometimes hinging on the goodness of other human beings to make it possible for them to have a new life. This hope is daily bread. It supports and sustains them in their time of suffering. This hope literally keeps uprooted persons alive.

Even so, the uprooted rekindle the hope which is in Christ. Beyond tribulation there is relief from suffering. Beyond persecution in repressive nation states, there will be liberation. Beyond hunger, there will be bread for all. Beyond homelessness there will be a secure home. Beyond battles and bloodshed, there will be peace. Beyond those principalities and powers that stunt and thwart and cut short human life, there will be "shalom."

Paul Tournier, whose book *A Place for You* led the first chapter of this study, writes of "the longing for perfection which sleeps deep in our own souls . . . . What is the meaning of this nostalgia for perfection which some admit and others hide, but which is inevitably there in every man and woman? It is our homesickness for Paradise. The place we are all looking for is the Paradise we have lost. The whole of humanity suffers from what we might call the 'Paradise Lost' complex."[6]

Uprooted people coming out of the distress of the clash of kingdoms of this world can provide a new view of the earth. They can enable all to gain a "spaceship" view of this precious planet which a single, whole community of people inhabit, rather than the "political map" view with nations divided by boundaries. They renew in hearts the vision of "shalom," of a world where all God's creation realizes the potential which has been placed within it. Through them the whole community can get a foretaste of that "paradise lost" which faith says stands glorious at the end of the human story.

Thus all are journeying, together with the world's uprooted persons, on the road from oppression to promise. The world's future hangs in the balance as Christians name the principalities and powers that have tyrannized and uprooted people. Christians address with whatever power they have those injustices which have rendered uprooted people powerless. Christians support uprooted persons in struggles toward land reform, job creation, self-determination, knowing that if such human rights are not secured for those uprooted now these rights in due time will not be secure for anyone. Whatever compassion is expressed toward them is but a taste of the compassionate community of God toward which rooted and uprooted persons move.

In all our journey and struggle, there is a hidden cry, "Come, Lord Jesus!" For we share the confident expectation that the reigns of this age will indeed become the reign of God in Christ.

FOOTNOTES

Chapter One

1. Paul Tournier, *A Place For You* (London: SOM Press Ltd.), 1968, Chapter I.
2. *Mexican Migration to the United States: Challenge to Christian Witness and National Policy*, a policy paper adopted by the General Assemblies of the Presbyterian Church in the United States and the United Presbyterian Church in the U.S.A., 1981, page 46. This paper has served as a major resource for this chapter.

Chapter Two

1. Adapted from *New Immigrants: Portraits in Passage*, by Thomas Bentz (New York: Pilgrim Press, 1981), pages 145-154.
2. "UNHCR Border Camps Save Khmer Lives," by Mark Malloch-Brown; *1981 World Refugee Survey*, page 25.
3. "Proud Tribesmen Shuttle Between War and Peace," by Edward Girardet, *Refugee Crisis*, reprinted from "The Christian Science Monitor" (Boston: The Christian Science Publishing Society, 1980), page 10.
4. A primary source for this section is "Brave Words and Stark Survival," by Mehr Kamal; *UNICEF News*, Issue 106, 1980/4, pages 18ff.
5. Adapted from *First Generation: In the Words of Twentiety-Century American Immigrants*, by June Namias (Boston: Beacon Press, 1978), pages 211-216.
6. Notes from personal interview with Rev. Aude Rentisi in Ramallah, March 28, 1981.
7. "Dateline: Lebanon," Published by Church World Service, New York, May 5, 1981 issue by Richard Butler, page 5.
8. "Somalia: not just a crisis . . . a disaster," by Edward Girardet; *Refugee Crisis*, page 14.
9. From the Africa Fund newsletter, by Jennifer Davis, executive secretary. (New York: The Africa Fund, n.d.)
10. Bentz, pages 108-117.
11. "Helping the World's Homeless," by Edward Girardet; *Refugee Crisis*, page 1.
12. See "Addressing the Needs of Women Refugees," by Margaret Carpenter, *1981 World Refugee Survey*, pages 42ff.
13. See *UNICEF News*, Issue 106, 1980/4, entitled "Children on the Move."

Chapter Three

1. *1981 World Refugee Survey*, p. 41.
2. Ibid., p. 40.
3. Quoted in Bentz, p. xvii.
4. The National Council of Churches of Christ in the U.S.A. adopted such a policy statement in 1981. Denominations adopting statements include

the United Methodist Church, the United Church of Christ, the Lutheran Council in the U.S.A., the Mennonite Central Committee, the United Presbyterian Church in the U.S.A., the Presbyterian Church in the U.S. Copies of these statements can be obtained directly from the organizations' offices.

5. Frederick A. Norwood, *Strangers and Exiles: A History of Religious Refugees*, (Nashville: Abingdon Press, 1969). Vol. 2, p. 443.

Chapter Four

1. Jack Nelson, "Land and Justice"; *The Christian Rural Mission in the 1980's—A Call to Liberation and Development of Peoples* (published by Agricultural Missions, New York, 1979), p. 83.
2. "Navajos vs. Hopis: A Battle Over Land"; *Newsweek*, Sept. 21, 1981, p. 12.
3. Jack A. Nelson, *Hunger for Justice: The Politics of Faith* (Maryknoll, N.Y.: Orbis Books, 1980), p. 13.
4. From address by Charles R. Avila, at Agricultural Mission Consultation in Jayuya, Puerto Rico, April 16-19, 1979.
5. From report prepared by David A. Sebrepena, "The Impact of Private and Voluntary Aid Projects on the Self-Reliance and Empowerment of People in the Philippines" (mimeographed). p. 3f.
6. Avila, op. cit.
7. Bentz, p. 171.
8. Michael Maggie, "Shifting Sands of U.S. Immigration Policy Trap Salvadoran Refugees," from Church World Service *Refugees and Human Rights Newsletter*, Winter 1981, p. 19.
9. *New York Times*, March 15, 1980, quoted in Philip Wheaton, *Agrarian Reform in El Salvador: A Program of Rural Pacification* (Washington, D.C.: EPICA TASK FORCE, n.d.), p. 19.
10. Wheaton, op. cit., p. 13f.
11. Jack Nelson, "Hunger and the Crisis in American Agriculture," *This Land is Our Land: Portraits of the Struggle for Land, Food and Justice*, (New York: Clergy and Laity Concerned, n.d.), p. 3.
12. Wendell Berry, *The Unsettling of America: Culture and Agriculture*, (New York: Avon Books, 1977) reprinted by permission of Sierra Book Club, p. 33.
13. See Helen Matthews Lewis, Linda Johnson and Dan Askins, editors, *Colonialism in Modern America: The Appalachian Case*, (Beene, N.C.: Appalachian Consortium Press, 1978).
14. *Land Use, Issue 13*, Department of Church and Society, United Church of Canada, Sept. 1978.
15. Quoted in Gaspa Langella, "Salvador Poor: God's Sacrament?" *Presbyterian Survey*, Sept. 1981, p. 12.
16. Quoted in "Special Focus: Refugees from El Salvador and Guatemala: Action Guidelines for Canadian Churches" (Toronto: The Inter-Church Committee for Refugees, 1981), p. 6.
17. *North/South: A Programme for Survival*, Report of Independent Commission on International Development Issues (Cambridge, Mass.; the MIT Press, 1980), p. 95.

18.　*The Christian Rural Mission in the 1980's*, p. 3f.
19.　Ibid, (adapted from) p. 107f.

Chapter Five

1.　Bentz, p. 65f.
2.　*North/South*, p. 112.
3.　Peter A. Sohey, " 'Black Boat People' Founder on the Shoals of U.S. Policy," *Refugees and Human Rights Newsletter*, Church World Service, Winter 1981, p. 4.
4.　Peter Applebome, *New York Times*, Oct. 12, 1980, Section 12, p. 48f. Quoted in *Immigrants, Refugees and U.S. Policy*, Grant S. McClellan, Ed. the Reference Shelf, Vol. 52, No. 6 (New York: The H.W. Wilson Co., 1981) p. 41.
5.　*The Politics of People*, Issue 9, Department of Church in Society, United Church of Canada, May 1975.
6.　Interview in "Racism and Refugees," issue of *Response-Ability*, published by Division of Corporate and Social Mission, Presbyterian Church in the United States, Spring 1981, No. 11, p. 11.

Chapter Six

1.　Script for documentary film, "When a Factory Closes," by John Raines and Lenora Berson, Center of Ethics and Social Policy, Philadelphia, Pa., p. 4.
2.　Dial Torgerson, "America's Urban Wastelands," *Los Angeles Times*, Jan. 15, 1973, p. 1, 16-17. Quoted in *Crisis in Urban Housing*, edited by Grant S. McClellan, pp. 29-31.
3.　*Poor Kids*, a report by the National Council of Welfare on Children in Poverty in Canada, March 1975, p. 8-9.
4.　Joseph P. Fried, *Housing Crisis, U.S.A.*, Prager, 1971, pp. 229-232. Quoted in McClennan, op. cit., p. 239f.
5.　Information for this section has been secured from Lenore E. Walker, *The Battered Woman*, New York: Harper and Row, 1979.
6.　John G. Hubbell, "Father Ritter's Convenant," in *Reader's Digest*, October 1980, reprint.
7.　Much of the information for this section has been secured from Lillian Ambrosino, *Runaways*, Boston: Beacon Press, 1971.
8.　Article in *Atlanta Journal and Constitution*, Jan. 3, 1981, p. 2.
9.　Loretta Schwartz-Nobel, "Starving in the Shadow of Plenty"; in *Mother Jones*, Sept.-Oct. 1981, p. 48f.

Chapter Seven

1.　Quoted in Frederick A. Norwood, *Strangers and Exiles: A History of Religious Refugees*, (Nashville, Abingdon Press, 1969). Vol. II, p. 477.
2.　Roy Sano, "Our Faith and Refugee Resettlement," *Theological Reflections on Refugees*, published by Church World Service, p. 12.

3. Norwood, op. cit., p. 474f.
4. H. Richard Niebuhr, *The Meaning of Revelation*, p. 116. Quoted in "Immigrant Churches and Human Community," *The Presbyterian Outlook*, March 1, 1982, p. 5.
5. "Refugees and Immigration: the Liberty of Statutes," *Church and Society*, January-February 1982, pp. 14-19.
6. Tournier, op. cit., p. 38.